I0558959

BECOMING YOUR OWN QUANTUM ALCHEMIST MASTER

ROSALÍA QUINTANA

TecnoTur
Publishing
Is there a book inside you?

Becoming Your Own Quantum Alchemist Master

Remembering your SOUL, divinity, multidimensionality, and infinite potential.
Uniting the East, West, North, and South

Information received from the Cosmic Consciousness and my Guides

Written by: Rosalía Quintana

Quantum Alchemist Master ™

ISBN for the print book

979-8-9905171-2-7

ISBN for the ebook:

979-8-9905171-3-4

ISBN for the audiobook:

979-8-9905171-4-1

Edited by: Ailýn Miguel and the editorial team at TecnoTur Publishing

© 2024 Rosalía Quintana. All rights reserved, according to US, Pan-American, International, Interplanetary, and Intergalactic conventions. No part of this book may be reproduced or transmitted without the explicit, written permission from the author, except in the case of brief quotations in reviews, with a link to QuantumAlchemistNow.com

Acknowledgements

Dear family, friends, ancestors, mentors, and the incredible publishing team,

As I reflect back on this journey, I am filled with an overwhelming sense of gratitude for the remarkable souls who have accompanied me on this transformative journey as a spiritual guide and author. Your presence in my life has been nothing short of a divine blessing, and I wish to express my heartfelt appreciation for the profound impact you've had on my path, I could have never done this alone.

To my dearest family and friends, to my ancestors and especially to my devoted wife and son, your unwavering support and boundless love have been everything to me and why this is possible. Your belief in my aspirations, your patience in the face of my challenges, your unwavering encouragement through every twist and turn, and your belief in my soul have been my fuel. In your LOVE, I find the strength to speak my truth, and for that and many more reasons, my heart is filled with eternal gratitude for accompanying me on this journey.

To my mentors, thank you for lighting my path in my moments of darkness. Your wisdom, your illuminating insights, patience and your unwavering faith and guidance have been a compass on this profound journey. I thank your wisdom and cherish the immeasurable lessons you've imparted.

To my dedicated publisher and editor, your commitment has transmuted my words into a symphony of the soul. Your unyielding dedication to manifest my vision and your tireless efforts in bringing this book to life have been a catalyst to bring this from the formless into the form. I am truly humbled by your collaborative spirit and the magic you've woven into these pages. To all those who lent their expertise and passion to this project, your collective effort has breathed life into this dream. Each one of you has played an indispensable role in the manifestation of this book and my deepest desire is that its message touches the hearts and souls of all who encounter it. You have etched your presence onto this beautiful chapter of my life, and I hold dear the memories and shared experiences that have enriched my journey.

Thank you for being the guiding lights, the pillars of strength, and the wellspring of inspiration on this extraordinary odyssey. As I look forward to the adventures that lie ahead, I carry your love, support, and wisdom with me as a cherished treasure.

With a profound love,
Rosalía Quintana

CONTENTS

INTRODUCTION

This story is about a human who forgot her connection to her SOUL, divinity, her connection to Source, her multidimensionality, and infinite potential, and how she remembered some of it and the exact steps she took to get there. She was tired of asking herself the deeper questions in life, going to different seminars, paying thousands of dollars, and reading books of all sorts, including subjects such as money, manifestation, spirituality, and more. She knew others had done it and that she could do it too but she didn't know how, she was always looking for answers outside of herself, until she decided to go within and discovered a whole other world existed there. She was able to find her direct connection to Source, consciousness, guides, ancient teachings, Akashic Records, other dimensions, beings, remember past, parallel lives, access different timelines and much more through her heart.

«In mystical traditions, it is one's own readiness that makes experiences exoteric or esoteric. The secret isn't that you are not being told. The secret is that you're not able to hear.» - Ram Dass

She knew that it was possible, she always felt like there was more information or a greater truth to be shared and that is what she will be sharing with you in this book, from her perspective and her own journey, not to force it upon anyone but to share from her heart to yours, her ever changing and evolving level of consciousness and perspective. Her goal is to make sacred knowledge available and easy to understand. She discovered it for herself, changed her perspective of her inner world first and therefore the outside world started to change and noticed all the clues and breadcrumbs that were always there for her to help her remember her true divinity all along from caves, ancient to current texts, previous teachers, papyrus, tombs, sacred geometry, and much more. As she was able to remember and connect, she felt tremendous honor as she was standing on the shoulders of giants and learning from knowledge that has been shared since the beginning of time for humanity to build from it and continue learning and expanding our consciousness, species, awareness and understanding of this spirit-human journey. I invite you to approach the information in this book and elsewhere with a curious mindset. Using the understanding and perspective of others to guide you to look within in order to make your own progress and continue the expansion of consciousness.

«The truth has never denied the seeker. It is the seeker who has denied the truth.» - Unknown

She is of Cuban descent, and as she used to say in Castilian («Spanish»), she was set out to find out *«Por donde le entra el agua al coco?»*. This saying refers to how water enters a coconut and the meaning of the water in this case was sacred knowledge, Source, the unknown, the great mystery, etc. No, she does not have the answers to the great mystery, all of life's questions or Source. What she does have is the story telling of her own journey and what she has found to share with you with the hopes that may serve you in your own journey. She is a student just like you, witnessing the great mystery and the divine plan unfold before her every single day in the eternal present moment. This book is not a self-help book. It is a self-empowerment book and it is my intention that you awaken to the infinite, love, divine, co-creator, sovereign being that you are. Together we can build the rainbow bridge between heaven and earth.

There is nothing she knows that you don't. She is here to share her extremely limited perspective and her lens of perception from her own experience. She felt for a long time that most of humanity is the allegory of Plato's cave as she experienced that herself. Exiting this cave is an opportunity you will have after reading this book. Take what serves and resonates with you and leave the rest.

«Recognize that unlearning is the highest form of learning.» - Rumi

This book is being shared with the world with the intention that no one else forgets their soul, divine eternal being, infinite potential and multidimensionality, to help you find peace and love within yourself and others and therefore in the world.

«Man does not have a soul. He is a soul. He has a body.» - C.S. Lewis

Another one of my intentions is to help you remember and find this out by yourself by looking within and holding the mirror reflecting back that you are your own masters, gurus, and Source itself, it is an invitation to look within, and embody your greatness.

«We are stars wrapped in skin. The light you are seeking has always been within.» - Rumi

The intention is also to unite the east, west, north, and south, to bring love, awareness, consciousness, and peace into this world by sharing and respecting each of our journeys and stories and learn from each other. This also includes a request for a 10-year peace treaty that could prevent a future catastrophe. I highly encourage you to read to the end despite the differences in ideas and points of view. If it came across your path there must be a reason for it. There are no coincidences. Please help us spread the message by sharing it if it helped you on your journey. Help us spread LOVE!

This is not something limited to only a few or anyone

special; this is our birthright, and we all have access to this at any time.

«The kingdom of heaven is within you and whosoever shall know himself shall find it» - Egyptian *Book of the Dead*

It is time to break the cage and stop giving your power away to external sources. You are the master; you are the guru; you are the fifth element. You are who you have been looking for all along; you are the Messiah; you are the second coming of Christ; you are the universe and the universe is you. The answers are inside of you. Are you ready to step into your true potential? Are you ready to embark on a beautiful journey of remembrance that will most likely challenge everything you currently believe in and everything we have always been taught by society, parents, religion, the government, everything, and everyone else that surrounds us?

«Close both eyes to see with the other eye.» - Rumi

I would like to request that you leave judgment and your rational mind aside; connect with your heart, your intuition, your soul and let that be the guiding force to receive, interpret, and discern this information.

«The cosmos is also within us, we're made of star-stuff. We are a way for the cosmos, to know itself.» Carl Sagan's *See you on the other side...*

CHAPTER 1

DISCONNECTING FROM THE DIVINE

FORGETTING YOUR TRUE ESSENCE

From my limited and ever-changing perspective, I feel humans of course including myself have lost connection with their soul and spiritual Source? Take a moment to journey with me through a short synopsis of human history, where we'll explore a profound shift in our connection to the divine, a connection that has been with us since the dawn of time. From ancient beliefs to our modern disconnect. In the earliest days, humans looked to the heavens and the earth with wonder and reverence. Rocks, trees, animals, everything was thought to have a soul, spirit, consciousness, life force running through it. Over time, our spiritual connection evolved and eventually with the rise of major world religions. This spiritual connection shaped our art, music, literature, and even our understanding of our place in the world. As the centuries passed, a shift began. With the advent of science and rationalism our focus turned from faith to reason.

So, I invite you to keep an open mind and be open to look at other perspectives. Do you think you are your body, your gender, your religion, your ethnicity, your race, your profession, your role in society? Do you think you are destined to be born, study, get married, have children, work, retire, die and accept what your current beliefs and limitations are about your perceived reality and that of the world as the only truth or possibility? There is so much to discover and this book is a good place to start questioning everything, even everything I mention here. In my opinion, mankind's search for happiness is the search or remembrance of itself. The discovery of the true self, the soul, the higher self, Christ's consciousness within oneself. It is not just for people who have undergone many years of spiritual practice but it is available to everyone at all times. It is all about shifting your perspective and focusing your awareness. You are infinite consciousness in human form becoming aware of itself by dissolving the illusion, the layers, the programming, and going within.

«I... a universe of atoms, an atom in the universe.» - Richard Feynman

Once the veils and illusions begin to fall you begin to recognize the programming of the human psyche and stop feeding the programming that has been in place for eons. You have all the power but do you know how powerful you really are? There has been a lot of effort and resources to keep you from finding your true power.

We go through infinite layers of consciousness or awareness, from identifying with the fractal our soul has as a body and a particular perception of reality ever changing. To identify with a gender, race, ethnicity, your line of work, your community, your preferred sports team, your role in society, the country or state in which you live, to your contributions with the soul family with which you decided to incarnate. To an even broader perspective to all the people you come in contact with, to all of humanity as a species. We are infinite fractals of the whole, fractals of our own soul spread across all timelines, fractals of group soul and families. It's a ripple effect and the golden rule very well applies here because essentially, we are all one and love is the principle guiding force. It's like being a Matryoshka doll also known as stacking dolls that is one big doll and has many little ones inside of it. You are free to explore all spectrums of light, but the underlying permanence of your eternal divinity and love essence remains for all of eternity expressed in infinite forms and formlessness. Visible and invisible, animate and inanimate, through infinite dimensions. If you could imagine the infinity symbol in constant motion for all of eternity, ever changing, ever evolving, ever expanding. You begin to recognize and honor your infinite, eternal, divine soul, and Source itself in infinite forms of expression.

I also invite you to think of it this way: one Source, one infinite consciousness as one infinite brain, with the two halves as male and female. We humans are individual neurons in this brain. We each perceive and experience things differently according to the information and conditioning that has been passed down to us from other neurons we come in contact with in the process of synapses or communication between neurons. These being your parents, grandparents, society, life experiences, etc. However, we are not only limited to this, we can access the entire brain because we are also the entire brain as well as the neurons in it. It just happens each neuron has its own set of codes and information to share with each other and the world. These neurons have the capacity to think individually, process thought, and bring it from the formless to the form. So, what I invite you to do is to be open to communicating with other neurons, see what they have to say, they have information you may not have or may not have been exposed to. Listen, use discernment and think: Will this information assist me in creating new neural pathways that would add to my growth or capabilities and capacity as a neuron to coexist in this one brain, this one consciousness? If we started to work together more, listen and respect each other's truths or perceptions and use this to assist us, to bring forth a map of consciousness, to share with each other all neurons once they reach a certain level of awareness, we would have access to this map leading us to access the full capacity of our brain, creating with more love and consciousness and not forgetting to only create from the brain but also connect the heart as one with the process. Now, where do I think we are in this process? I believe we are only getting started and being open to bridge the form and formless together. I feel it is imperative to have at any given time infinite levels of consciousness and awareness to thrive and survive as a species. Most of this information is passed down through storytelling and books in previous times and now through social media such as podcasts and other forms. Also, music and art have always been beautiful forms of expression of different states of consciousness. There is at least one thing we can use from every religion, every race, every gender, every species, not only in the universe but in the multiverse, to collaborate in elaborating this map of accessing a bigger part of our consciousness and I don't believe one individual neuron can do this, and I'm referring to an individual human, I believe most of us are doing the best we can by sharing our insights but we get too much criticism and push back from the others, there is probably much more that could be shared in a more supportive environment. It is my belief that as individuals, we are only able to access infinity 0.0000001 of our actual capacity at this time in regards to the totality of the available consciousness for interaction, learning, and creation. It is my opinion that we are beginning to realize that alone, we cannot accomplish more than we can together as a collective, so will we come together not only for our individual good but for the highest good of the whole?

Once you begin to recognize the oneness of Source expressing itself in many unique ways to create this beautiful multiverse and we all get to experience creation together as one. Once this occurs you are more intentional with your choices, your thoughts, your responses and your respect for all life forms, your love and compassion for self and others. How do you think this information will impact the economy, the politics, the fear instilled in humanity since the beginning of time, how will this change our individual and collective reality when each person becomes a sovereign being, without needing any saving, without needing to become anything because you have always been the whole, the totality. What if you were an eternal superhero and simply the villains (other forms with less consciousness or a different agenda other than love) have confused you and caused you to forget due to external programming and beliefs?

«The hostile forces have a certain self-chosen [teaching] function; it is to test the condition of the individual, of the work, of the earth itself and their readiness for the spiritual descent and fulfillment.» - Sri Aurobindo

No one can do this inner alchemy, this alignment with your soul, this meeting of the minds with consciousness and awareness.

«Ultimately, it is about engaging in the Great Work to anchor the soul firmly in your being (living in the Divine) and make it the master instead of your conditioned ego-personality running the show, which these forces can easily manipulate.» - Berhard Guenther

So how will you choose to employ your free will, could there be more to us, to reality, to humanity, to the universe than what we have been told?

What if you are limitless, boundless, and Source itself.

«A teacher is never a giver of truth-he is a guide, a pointer to the truth that each student must find for himself.» - Bruce Lee

You must first become aware of your limiting beliefs,

perceived boundaries and limitations, and the false programming of the matrix which I see as simple as a set of beliefs and programming supported by our individual and collective thoughts, beliefs, and actions, and current perspective. This can be changed, molded, altered but first you must become aware of it, otherwise how can you change something you don't know it exists or its not benefiting you. No, this book won't be about conspiracy theories but I can't turn a blind eye to programming that is affecting our entire system of mind, body and spirit. How can you become aware of what is no longer serving us as a humanity? example a simple one that you must change your food choices because it's making you sick? Do you need to wait for a cancer or an illness to show you or can we proactively become aware and be active participants of the change, let's not keep feeding the big pharma and big corporations use your discernment and go within. This false programming is nothing to be afraid of. It is just there to serve as contrast for you to recognize your true self and your greatness. Once you do, you transcend all veils of illusion and the false programming falls apart it no longer has power over you and of course in turn, you no longer feed into that system of set of beliefs. The more of us that awaken to our true self, the sooner we will birth a new individual and collective reality for all.

«Your soul already knows the answer. You just have to be quiet enough to hear it, and brave enough to listen.» - Stacie Martin

Back to forgetting your true essence, logic became our

compass, and many of us began to dismiss spirituality as superstitious, science fiction, magic, witchcraft, mental health disorders, etc. Can you feel how this altered our connection to the divine, to your own soul, higher self and Source itself? The impact of the modern world, the industrial revolution, technological advancements, etc. made our lives easier, but also more disconnected from nature and each other. Cities grew, materialism flourished, and our spiritual essence seemed to fade. We also became disconnected from our feelings. We numbed ourselves, avoiding the deep questions that once led us closer to our divinity. The loss of our spiritual connection has had profound consequences. It's left us grappling with emptiness, anxiety, depression, addiction, mental health, unbalance and other issues including environmental degradation, social inequality, and more. Our sense of unity and purpose has been shattered. The connection with the divine is still within us, waiting to be rediscovered. At least that is my perception. I am just continuing to learn, unlearn, relearn, alongside you, evolve, understand. I am here to be of service to love as a humble teacher and student of life. I am trying to figure it out as I go along just like you. I am honored to share my limited piece with you with love with the hopes that anything here may serve all those that come in contact with it.

How beautiful it is that we have so many paths to choose from! We can meditate, pray, journal, practice yoga, do plant medicine, mantras, art and creativity, access our Akashic Records, music, and energy work and many, many other modalities embrace in mindfulness to connect with our inner selves. We can explore nature, where the spirit of life dances in everything. For some, therapy, counseling, community can be a guiding light, and for others, acts of kindness and community service can rekindle that sense of divine connection. Our journey from the earliest days of human history to our current disconnected state is complex, but it's never too late to find our way back home.

By embracing spiritual practices, reconnecting with nature, seeking support, and engaging in acts of kindness, forgiveness, opening your heart and connecting to your intuition to Source within yourself, we can heal the spiritual rift that has grown within us. We can overcome the illusion of separation. Together we can remember our roots and move toward a more connected, fulfilling existence. The divine is waiting, and all we need to do is take that first step and look within, quiet the outside, take away the anesthesia, take away the blindfold, get out of your comfort zone find courage and look within to reconnect with your eternal soul, Source, consciousness, and universal oneness.

«The total number of minds in the universe is one. In fact, consciousness is a singularity phasing within all beings.» - Erwin Schrodinger

CHAPTER 2

THE JOURNEY OF SELF-DISCOVERY

REDISCOVERING THE SOUL

W hat can trigger a spiritual awakening and the stages of a spiritual awakening, if you have been on your spiritual journey for a while you may already be familiar with what can trigger a spiritual awakening and the different stages of spiritual awakening, the work of Carl Jung, *The Hero's Journey*, the alchemical process, the 12 Labors of Hercules and how they can be compared to the spiritual and alchemical journey. If so you may choose to get a refresher or skip this chapter all together. For those of you who have not heard of some of these, you are in for a treat and you will gain a better understanding of how our spirit-human journey is connected to all these processes.

What can trigger a spiritual awakening:

Various life events and experiences can trigger a spiritual awakening or serve as catalysts for a deepening of one's spiritual journey.

Illness or Health Crisis: A serious illness, especially one that poses a life-threatening situation, can prompt individuals to reevaluate their priorities, seek deeper meaning, and explore their spiritual beliefs and practices.

Near-Death Experience (NDE): Surviving a near-death experience, where individuals feel a profound sense of leaving their physical bodies and entering a different realm, often leads to spiritual awakenings as they grapple with questions about the nature of existence and the afterlife.

Divorce or Relationship Breakdown: The dissolution of a long-term relationship or marriage can be a major life upheaval that prompts individuals to reflect on their sense of self, purpose, and the nature of love and connection.

Loss of a Loved One: Grief and the loss of someone close can lead to a deep questioning of life's impermanence and the search for comfort and understanding in spirituality.

Sudden and Spontaneous Awakening: Some individuals may experience a spiritual awakening seemingly out of nowhere, often referred to as a «sudden enlightenment» or «spontaneous awakening.» These experiences can be triggered by a random event, a moment of deep insight, or simply a profound shift in consciousness.

Existential Crisis: A crisis of existential nature, where individuals grapple with questions about the meaning and purpose of life, can push them towards a spiritual journey in search of answers and understanding.

Major Life Transition: Significant life changes like retirement, relocation, or career shifts can prompt individuals to reevaluate their values and goals, leading to spiritual exploration.

Birth of a Child: The birth of a child can inspire profound shifts in perspective, as individuals contemplate the miracle of life and their roles as parents, often leading to spiritual exploration.

Natural Disasters or Traumatic Events: Living through natural disasters or traumatic events can prompt individuals to seek solace, meaning, and healing in spirituality as they cope with the aftermath.

Travel and Cultural Exposure: Immersion in different cultures, traditions, or spiritual practices during travel can open one's eyes to diverse spiritual beliefs and philosophies, triggering a desire for deeper exploration.

Loss of Material Wealth: A sudden loss of material wealth or financial security can lead to a reevaluation of one's relationship with materialism and the pursuit of more spiritual values.

Retirement: Entering retirement can provide individuals with the time and space to explore their inner selves, contemplate life's purpose, and deepen their spiritual practices.

It's important to note that a spiritual awakening can be a highly personal and subjective experience.

While these events can serve as catalysts, the journey and timing of a spiritual awakening are unique to each individual. Some may experience gradual shifts, while others may undergo sudden and profound transformations. Ultimately, these triggers can lead to a deeper understanding of oneself, a connection to higher consciousness, and a sense of purpose and meaning in life.

Focusing and turning inward for alchemy, remembrance, and awakening

External distraction detox:

Such as meditation, breathwork, silence retreat, darkness retreat, cocoon meditations, prayer, writing, art, mantras, plant medicine, yoga, qigong, tai-chi, sensory deprivation tanks, alone time anywhere you can be by yourself sitting under a tree or nature immersion or walks in nature by yourself, etc.

The stages of a spiritual awakening:

Egg Stage - The Seed of Awakening: Much like the egg of a butterfly, a spiritual awakening begins with a tiny seed planted deep within. This seed represents the initial curiosity or yearning for something more profound in life, often triggered by life's challenges or questions about one's purpose.

Caterpillar Stage - The Search for Meaning: As the caterpillar emerges from the egg, you embark on a quest for answers and deeper understanding. You voraciously consume knowledge and experiences, seeking meaning and purpose in the world around you.

Cocoon Stage - The Spiritual Crisis: The cocoon stage is where you undergo a profound internal transformation. Much like the caterpillar encased in its cocoon, you may find yourself isolated or in a state of spiritual crisis. This period can be filled with confusion, emotional turmoil, and a sense of being in the dark, mirroring the cocoon's darkness.

Metamorphosis Stage - Inner Alchemy: Within the cocoon, your inner alchemy unfolds. Just as the caterpillar undergoes a complete metamorphosis, your old self begins to dissolve, and profound changes occur on every level – mentally, emotionally, and spiritually. This is a time of inner growth and self-discovery.

Emergence Stage - The Butterfly's Revelation: Finally, after a patient and transformative journey, you emerge as a butterfly from your cocoon. Like the butterfly spreading its wings for the first time, you unveil your true self. You experience a sense of inner freedom, love, and interconnectedness with all of creation.

Flight Stage - Embracing Spiritual Freedom: As a butterfly takes flight, you soar into the world with newfound wisdom and awareness. You share your inner light and love, inspiring others and contributing positively to the collective consciousness.

Life Cycle - Continuous Growth: Similar to a butterfly's ongoing cycles of life, death, and rebirth, your spiritual journey becomes a continuous process of growth and evolution. You may experience multiple awakenings and transformations throughout your life, each deepening your connection with the divine and expanding your consciousness.

Just as nature guides the butterfly through these stages, the universe gently guides you on your spiritual awakening journey. Embrace the beauty and wisdom of this process, for it leads you toward your true self and a deeper connection with the universe. Trust in the unfolding of your own unique path, knowing that, like the butterfly, you are destined to reveal your inner beauty and purpose.

«The butterfly does not look back at the caterpillar in shame, just as you should not look back at your past in shame. Your past was part of your own transformation.» - Anthony Gucciardi

LOOKING at the lens of self-discovery through the wisdom of the great Swiss psychologist Carl Jung, who discerned the profound impacts of our modern materialistic world. Today's pursuits of money, pleasure, fame, and power have led many of us into a labyrinth of anxiety, depression, suffering, and loneliness.

Rediscovering the Soul

Jung's insights beckon us to return to the search for our soul, to restore our connection with our inner self. Our true personality consists of both conscious and unconscious lives, and navigating this intricate labyrinth is our journey of psychological maturation. This path, known as the individuation process, leads us toward tranquility and wholeness, not mere perfection.

The Stages of Life

In Jung's eyes, the journey comprises two vital stages. The first half of life immerses us in the external world – work, education, relationships. We must endure daily life and hard work, which solidifies our personality. Here, nature nourishes us, and our connection to the soil reminds us not to lose ourselves in abstract thinking.

The second half of life shifts our focus inward. The world of the inner life is as boundless as the outer, yet many neglect this realm and fall into crisis. Jung valued simple acts that anchor us in reality, guiding us to align both worlds and avoid the conformity that often leads to self-alienation.

The Soul's Longing

When we're confronted with life's crushing problems, we search desperately for our soul. The search is a solitary task, and the soul, restless, keeps stirring within us. However, these problems become incentives to undertake soul work. As Jung wisely observed, the loss of the soul leads to a sense of meaninglessness.

Techniques for Self-Knowledge

Jung offers the technique of active imagination, where you engage in dialogue with different parts of yourself that reside in the unconscious. It's a conscious dreaming experience that led him to create *The Red Book*, a significant contribution to humanity. Your way to the soul is your own. Look within to find your path, and you may experience synchronicities – those meaningful patterns that connect the inner world with external reality.

Archetypes and Integration

Jung identified universal archetypes present in the collective unconscious of all humans, such as The Shadow, The Anima/Animus, The Self, The Persona, and The Trickster. Awareness of these archetypes helps with integration and personal growth.

The Shadow

The shadow is not an enemy but a hidden ally waiting to be discovered. It represents those repressed aspects of our psyche that we often deem unacceptable fears, desires, instincts. The shadow may contain dark elements like aggression and jealousy, but it also harbors creativity and passion. To deny the shadow is to fragment our being. Yet, embracing it leads to wholeness. Through active imagination and dream analysis, we can learn to recognize and accept our shadow. Remember, the shadow can be a collective phenomenon too, present in groups, societies, and cultures, influencing social conflicts.

The Anima/Animus: The Anima and Animus symbolize the opposite gender traits within us all. In men, the Anima represents the female psychological tendencies, the Source of life, enriched with feelings, moods, and fantasies. When not integrated, we may feel lifeless and depressed. In women, the Animus symbolizes male psychological tendencies, the Source of meaning and qualities like initiative and courage. Integrating the Anima and Animus enriches our lives, making the unconscious conscious. This integration is achieved by taking our unconscious content seriously and manifesting it through creative work like painting, writing, music, sculpture or other art forms.

«Artistic practice keeps us oriented to creation and keeps reconnecting us to the greater self within.» - Michael Mead

The Self: The Unity of the Psyche

The Self, represents the unity of the psyche, the culmination of Jung's individuation process. It's a concept that transcends the ego, embodying the integration of all aspects of our personality. The journey to the Self is the path to wholeness. It's a merging of opposites, an acknowledgment of our light and dark sides. The Self is the spiritual center that gives us a sense of meaning and coherence. Embrace it, for it's the true mirror of our existence.

Rediscovering the Soul

The Persona is the social mask we wear, the aspect molded by societal expectations and norms. While it helps us navigate the world, an over-reliance on the Persona can detach us from our true selves. Let us not forget who we are behind our masks. Recognize the Persona, but also transcend it. Be aware of the roles you play but remain connected to your authentic self, your higher self, your soul. The balance between the Persona and the authentic Self is a delicate dance of existence.

The Trickster: The Disruptor of Order

Lastly, the Trickster, an archetype that delights and challenges us. This mischievous figure disrupts order and convention, symbolizing the creative and transformative aspects of the psyche. Embrace the Trickster within. Allow it to challenge the status quo in your life, sparking creativity and growth. The Trickster's unpredictability is not a menace but an invitation to explore new possibilities.

These archetypes are keys to unlocking the doors of self-understanding. They are reflections in the cosmic mirror, guiding us to embrace all facets of our being. As we navigate our unique paths, let these concepts light our way, embracing the Shadow, integrating the Anima and Animus, recognizing the Persona, journeying to the Self, and dancing with the Trickster. Continue this great adventure of self-discovery, and may you find wisdom, love, and fulfillment in the infinite depths of your soul.

The Jungian perspective offers us a profound roadmap

for understanding ourselves and our place in the world. Open your hearts and go back and forth until you find that hidden door within your soul, opening into the cosmic consciousness that was there long before your ego arrived. Remember, the longest distance may be between our heart and our minds. Let us bridge that distance and move toward a more fulfilled existence. The path to the self is an integration of opposites, a union of light and dark. Embrace it, for it is the journey of life.

Let us now venture into the profound and transformative Hero's Journey, a universal pattern that Carl Jung's work inspired, and that many scholars, like Joseph Campbell, have further explored.

The Hero's Journey: A Path to Transformation

The Hero's Journey is a sacred path that resonates within all human souls, a pattern found in mythologies, stories, and the deep wellsprings of our own lives. It symbolizes our quest for self-realization, for unlocking our innermost potential, and for becoming who we truly are.

The Call to Adventure: The Journey begins

The Hero's Journey starts with a call. It might be a whisper from within, a longing for something more, or a sudden life event that shatters our complacency. This call beckons us to leave the known world behind and embark on a journey into the unknown. Are you hearing this call?

Refusal of the Call: Resistance and Fear

At times, fear and doubt might hold us back. We may resist the call, clinging to the familiar and the comfortable. Yet, the soul yearns for growth, and the call persists, awaiting our courageous response.

Crossing the Threshold: Entering the Unknown

With courage and determination, we cross the threshold, entering the mysterious and magical world of transformation. It's a path filled with trials, challenges, and also gifts.

The Road of Trials: Growth through Challenges

The road of trials is not an easy path, but it's here that we find our strength, wisdom, and hidden talents. It's through facing our dragons, overcoming obstacles, that we grow and mature. Every challenge is a teacher, every struggle a step toward our true selves.

The Innermost Cave: Facing the Shadow

In the depths of the innermost cave, we face our shadow, our deepest fears, and unacknowledged parts. This is the crucible of transformation, where we embrace our wholeness and discover our hidden gold.

The Return: Bringing the Treasure Home

The final phase of the Hero's Journey is the return home, enriched with wisdom, love, and understanding. The hero brings back a treasure, a gift for the community, and a deeper connection to the self.

Embracing Your Hero's Journey

In my experience the Hero's Journey is not just a mythical pattern but a living reality in our lives. It's the adventure, filled with challenges, growth, discoveries, and profound transformations.

Do not fear the path; embrace it. For within you lies a hero waiting to be awakened. Answer the call, face your trials, discover your true self, and return with the precious treasure of wisdom and love. In the sacred dance of life, may your Hero's Journey illuminate your path, nourish your soul, and inspire those around you.

Now let us dive into the alchemical process, a deeply mystical and spiritual pursuit. Let's gently unravel this beautiful wisdom, for in my personal experience alchemy is not merely about transforming base metals into gold. It is a symbolic representation of our journey, transcending the limitations of our earthly existence.

The Alchemical Process: A Journey of Soul Transformation

In the sacred tradition of alchemy, the transformation of the soul is likened to the refinement of raw substances into pure gold. It is a metaphor for the individuation process that Carl Jung found deeply inspiring. This ancient wisdom beckons us to explore the depths of our inner world and discover the Divine spark within.

Prima Materia - The Primal Substance

In the alchemical journey, we start with the concept of Prima Materia, often symbolized as a formless, chaotic substance. It represents the raw material of the universe, the essence of all things. Just as the universe is made up of of diverse elements, the Prima Materia embodies the unity and potential within all of creation.

As we dive into our spiritual path, we can see our own lives as this Prima Materia, a blend of experiences, emotions, and energies waiting to be transformed and refined into something higher. It's a reminder that every aspect of our existence has the potential for transmutation and spiritual growth.

NIGREDO: The Blackening Stage

In this initial phase, the alchemical process begins with a disintegration of the known, a descent into darkness and chaos. It's akin to facing the shadow within, confronting our fears, illusions, and false identities. Just as the darkest hour precedes the dawn, this stage lays the groundwork for a profound transformation.

Albedo: The Whitening Stage

Emerging from the dark night of the soul, we enter the phase of purification and cleansing. In Albedo, the soul is washed and purified, like silver being refined. We shed our old patterns and beliefs, allowing our authentic self to emerge. In this stage of inner light, a deeper connection with the soul begins to grow.

The Alchemical Wedding - Union of Opposites

The Alchemical Wedding symbolizes the union of opposites, often depicted as the sacred marriage between the King and Queen. This union signifies the harmonization of masculine and feminine energies, the integration of light and shadow, and the coming together of the conscious and unconscious aspects of the self.

In our personal journey, the Alchemical Wedding represents our inner integration, a process of balancing our perceived dualities, resolving inner conflicts, and aligning with our true nature. It's about finding harmony within, which leads to a deeper connection with the universal energies.

Citrinitas: The Yellowing Stage

Citrinitas is the dawn of spiritual consciousness, the golden illumination of the mind and heart. It symbolizes wisdom, enlightenment, and the integration of opposites. Here, the masculine and feminine, the anima and animus, are united, and we begin to glimpse our Divine nature.

Rubedo: The Reddening Stage

The final stage, Rubedo, is the realization of the Philosopher's Stone, the symbol of wholeness and enlightenment. It's the union of the human with the Divine, the earthly with the eternal. This is the stage of Self-realization, where we recognize our inner Divinity and our connection with the All.

The Philosopher's Stone - Transmutation and Enlightenment

The Philosopher's Stone, often regarded as the pinnacle of alchemical achievement, is a mystical and elusive substance said to possess the power to transmute base metals, like mercury, into gold. It symbolizes spiritual enlightenment and the transformation of the human soul into a pure, divine state.

In our own spiritual awakening, the Philosopher's Stone mirrors the inner alchemy we undergo. It's about transmuting our ego-driven, "base" aspects into the gold of spiritual wisdom, compassion, and love. Just as the alchemist seeks the Philosopher's Stone, we seek to discover the divine essence within ourselves.

Remember, the journey toward the Philosopher's Stone is not about material wealth but the spiritual riches that come from inner transformation. It's about recognizing the interconnectedness of all life and aligning with the universal flow of energy. As you navigate your own spiritual path, keep these alchemical symbols in mind, and you'll find that the quest for inner gold is a journey well worth taking.

Your Alchemical Transformation

In my opinion the alchemical process is not a relic of the past but a living metaphor for our spiritual journey. It invites us to embrace our darkness, purify our hearts, awaken to wisdom, and realize our divine nature. Embrace the alchemy of your soul. Let the fires of transformation refine you. Let the waters of wisdom cleanse you. Let the air of under-standing elevate you, and let the earth of your body be the sacred vessel of your divine essence. May you become the gold that you seek, reflecting the love, wisdom, and unity within you.

«Alchemy has performed for me the great and invaluable service of providing material in which my experience could find sufficient room, and thereby made it possible for me to describe the individuation process at least in its essential aspects.» Carl Jung

How the 12 Labors of Hercules can be compared to the spiritual and alchemical journey

1. Slaying the Nemean Lion (Ego Death): Just as Hercules had to confront the invulnerable Nemean Lion, the spiritual journey often begins with a battle against the ego. Slaying the ego represents shedding the false self and embracing authenticity.
2. Slaying the nine-headed Lernaean Hydra (Overcoming Negative Habits): The Hydra represents our negative habits and addictions.

Like Hercules, we must confront and overcome these destructive patterns, which can multiply if left unchecked.

3. Capture of the Golden Hind of Artemis (Seeking Higher Truth): Hercules was tasked with capturing a sacred deer, symbolizing the pursuit of higher truths and spiritual knowledge. This parallels the spiritual journey's quest for enlightenment and wisdom.

4. Capture of the Erymanthian Boar (Taming the Mind): The wild boar represents the unruly mind. Taming the mind is essential in the spiritual journey, as it allows us to find inner peace and clarity.

5. Cleaning the Augean Stables (Purification): Hercules had to clean the seemingly insurmountable filth of King Augeas' stables in a single day. This labor symbolizes the process of inner purification and cleansing one's life of impurities.

6. Defeating the Stymphalian Birds (Overcoming Negative Thoughts): The Stymphalian Birds were fierce creatures that Hercules had to drive away with noise. Similarly, the spiritual journey involves battling and dispelling negative thoughts that hinder growth.

7. Capturing the Cretan Bull (Mastering Desires): Hercules had to capture a wild bull, representing the mastery of desires and impulses. This aligns

with the spiritual path's goal of transcending worldly desires.

8. Obtaining the Mares of Diomedes (Controlling Passion): Diomedes' man-eating horses symbolize unbridled passions. Taming them reflects the need to channel our emotions and desires for spiritual growth.

9. Obtaining the Belt of Hippolyta (Embracing Feminine Wisdom): Hercules had to obtain the belt of the Amazonian queen, Hippolyta. This labor signifies the integration of feminine wisdom, intuition, and nurturing qualities in the spiritual journey.

10. Capture of the Cattle of Geryon (Integration of Duality): Hercules had to gather the cattle belonging to Geryon, a three-bodied giant. This task reflects the spiritual journey's integration of dualities and the realization of unity.

11. Obtaining the Apples of the Hesperides (Attaining Enlightenment): To obtain the golden apples, Hercules had to seek the wisdom of the Hesperides. This labor mirrors the quest for enlightenment and the pursuit of spiritual knowledge.

12. Capture of Cerberus (Confronting Fear of Death): Hercules' final labor was capturing the three-headed dog guarding the underworld. This represents the ultimate confrontation of the fear of death, which is often a significant aspect of the spiritual journey.

.   .   .

JUST AS HERCULES' labors were trials leading to his apotheosis, the spiritual and alchemical journey involves facing inner challenges and transformations that lead to spiritual awakening and self-realization. Each labor corresponds to a stage of growth and evolution, ultimately leading to a more harmonious existence.

«To conquer the shadows that loom large, one must pierce through the illusionary veils and find strength in the truth that adversity is often a phantom, dissipating when faced with unwavering courage.» - Maya Angelou

CHAPTER 3

THE DEVELOPMENT PROCESS

GOING FROM PLANNING TO 2.0 AND BEYOND.

N ow that you have an overview of where I am going with this, I will break up these following chapters of my life from childhood to the present moment in the next chapter, but first I have to give you an overview for better understanding and foundation. I will share with you my journey and also the tools I used that greatly helped me transform my life with the hopes to motivate you to look within in your journey to find your own answers, your own truth and authenticity, again I do not hold any answers that impose a universal truth or answers to life's questions, I hold an ever-changing limited perspective of my own journey and from my heart I am looking to share it with the world so we can walk this journey together respecting each other and honoring each other truths and ever changing cycles, to inspire one another. I will talk about my life in comparison to the phases in the software development process. Why? Don't ask me. That's just how it came from my guides, my higher self and my intuition. I am no software developer of any kind. I did some basic research about some of the steps to be able to relate the information and if I get the phases wrong, please continue on as it is for informational purposes only and it makes it easier to explain the concepts. In this chapter, I will attempt to explain the development process so it can all make sense throughout the book.

I am aware that spirituality is a complex, ever evolving spiral, multi-dimensional concept that encompasses many different beliefs, practices, and experiences, so you may not necessarily agree with my view but it is definitely worth listening until the end. There are some golden nuggets in here, I promise you that. I consider myself an eternal student and I hope one of the things this book does is inspire you to speak and share your truth, your perspective with the world and hopefully I will have the honor of hearing about it and learning from each of you as well. It is an honor to walk the path and learn together.

The Planning, Analysis, and Design Phase

In the grand tapestry of existence, before we even draw our first breath, it is my perspective that there unfolds a mystical process, an adventure that our soul embarks upon. It's something I refer to as the pre-incarnation process, a series of phases leading up to our birth, where our soul consciously chooses to incarnate in a physical body. This concept of choosing to incarnate is profound and deeply personal. It's not a linear or uniform process; instead, it's unique to each of us. I believe that many elements contribute to this choice, including our soul's mission, karma, past life experiences, and the lessons we wish to explore in our current lifetime, our free will, and other unknown factors. Think of it as a collaborative effort, where your soul works in harmony with spiritual guides or other beings. Together, we select a suitable body and life circumstances, aligning everything for our highest good and the greater well-being of all involved. It can get a bit more complex than this when you consider past, present, future, multi-dimensions and parallel lives all coexisting at the same time which we will touch on more later in the book. Like a soul blueprint that consists of many multi-dimensional parts all existing at the same time and all contribute to the evolution and composition of the entire soul.

This idea is empowering and filled with purpose. By recognizing that we have actively chosen our life path and experiences, we reclaim responsibility for our growth and development. If you want to think of us as consciousness in action with the ability to create in the world of form. It's in our power to see our challenges and obstacles not as hindrances but as opportunities for learning, spiritual evolution, and co-creation of our reality. As my guides once showed me, responsibility has two separate words: response-ability, the ability to respond to life circumstances. The wise Maya Angelou once said:

«When you know better, you do better.»

As we grow in awareness and consciousness and learn to tap into our inner guidance, we become capable of making informed choices. Our path becomes clearer, and our journey more rewarding.

Before entering this physical realm, our soul forms agreements with other souls, crafting a soul contract filled with lessons and challenges tailored for our growth. While some may think these contracts are set in stone, I believe they are fluid, allowing for renegotiation, editing, alteration, and many possibilities exist at once. Please do not try to rationalize every word or idea in this book, this is for your soul to decode, surrender and allow for the process to occur, in due time you will integrate what you need. We can work with our spiritual guides to make necessary changes to our soul's contract, access our Akashic Records and other ways. The idea is to take charge, find purpose, choose to see from the lens of love, joy, and abundance, while recognizing the natural cycles and perspective of opposites that are integral to our growth and transformation. I recommend you watch the Disney movie *Soul* for another perspective or head onto our FREE resources tab on our website: quantumalchemist master.com.

For me, peace and contentment come from finding balance amidst all these moving parts and relishing the ever-present «now» moment. I love being open and letting the universe surprise me for my highest good as the observer of my experience. Life's human experience in my opinion is spiral, allowing for diverse lessons and experiences, none better or higher than the other, all just as energy in motion all essential for a full, rich human experience and our process of evolution as a species. In this journey, we must trust that everything is unfolding for our highest good, embracing both light and darkness, knowing that they are complementary in the cycles of life. Embrace the infinite possibilities for our existence is a beautiful dance, a harmonious melody composed by the universe, and we are the musicians playing the symphony of our lives. According to the author Lao Tzu (a name meaning «the old master»), the Tao is found where we would least expect it--not in the strong but in the weak; not in speech but in silence; not in doing but in «not-doing.» Wise yet worldly, spiritual yet practical, the Tao Te Ching.

The developing and testing phase

Life, in its endless wisdom and complexity, presents us with this process that I like to call the developing and testing phase. This phase, a continuous part of our existence, begins in the formative years of childhood and extends throughout our journey. In the early years, we're like computers running on software written by others. Our parents, teachers, media, and governments provide the coding that shapes our understanding of the world. Everything is external, and we often look outside ourselves for love, validation, and a sense of worth.

Sadly, this external programming can come with glitches: limiting beliefs, repetitive patterns, destructive behaviors, trauma and sometimes, limitations of our innate creativity. These glitches are not universal, of course, but they are common enough to be notable. The situation can become even more complicated if we add in the heavy burdens of addiction, trauma, abuse, or abandonment. How then is a child in this critical developmental phase supposed to thrive when the very code that's supposed to guide them has programming done by others?

The beauty of this phase is in its name: developing and testing. We are not passive recipients of this coding; we are active participants in life, capable of rewriting our software, debugging the system, and even installing new programs that align with our true selves. Of course, not as children but as we grow and develop in our journey.

We begin to recognize that we have the power to redefine our reality. We start to question the external influences and listen more to our inner wisdom. We learn to nurture our creativity, embrace our unique identity, and discard the limiting beliefs that no longer serve us. It's like upgrading our system to a version that resonates with our soul, with our soul's plan and blueprint according to the divine plan, one that empowers us to live authentically and love unconditionally.

This process is not always easy; it requires patience, forgiveness, self-love, self-compassion, self-awareness, and courage.

«Perhaps, we should learn to love ourselves so loudly, it silences our insecurities.» - Louise Kaufmann

It requires some of the previous processes explained prior including but not limited to Jung's individuation process, the hero journey and the alchemical process. It might mean facing painful memories or challenging deeply ingrained patterns. But the reward is an alignment with our true selves, a connection to our inner wisdom, and a life lived with purpose and joy. It is us going into the cocoon state and emerging as a butterfly by going within.

Remember that this developmental phase is not a stagnant state, but a journey of continuous growth and evolution. It's a path filled with opportunities for self-discovery, healing, and transformation. You have the power to rewrite your code, to create a life that reflects your deepest desires and highest aspirations. Take the wheel and steer your life in the direction you choose. You are the programmer of your reality, and the world awaits your unique and beautiful gifts.

From Alpha to ßeta Testing

Now the Alpha phase is the first phase of software testing that occurs after the development phase. During this phase, the software is tested by the development team to identify and fix any bugs or issues before releasing it to external testers or customers. The focus of the alpha phase is on finding glitches in the software and ensuring that it meets the intended functionality.

Here the external world begins wanting to fix us when we are already perfect just by merely existing and being ourselves as we are love and a spark and fractal of the divine. When I say «they» or «external world», I mean a more unconscious fractal or side of us that exists and helps to create both individual and collective reality. Therefore, I would love to encourage everyone to become conscious leaders and alchemists first of our own life and then of the world. It is a ripple effect. Do not underestimate how one soul can affect millions as we are all connected. If you want to think of us as individual neurons part of a bigger quantum neural brain or in this case consciousness. Therefore, if most neurons fire together with the thought of the idea of the new world, we want to create that new world together as the powerful co-creators that we are. This co-creation starts by awareness, self-love and finding inner harmony first and then we will reflect it in the material world.

Like Nikola Tesla said:

«We are all one. Only egos, beliefs, and fears separate us.»

In this phase, many of us don't fit in society, in current school systems, we don't fit in with the family and are often looked at as the black sheep. Simply for being different or wanting to follow the path less traveled. For being innovators, disruptors and wanting to create a better and different world where we can all express ourselves without restriction without being labeled or wanting to put us in a box or silence us. Here we try our best most of the time at least for a while to please others and try to fit in and lay low hoping we can make it. Then begins our descent into darkness. Also referred to as the dark night of the soul to me is not just a metaphor; it's a real stage that many of us experience on our spiritual journey. It's a time when the old ways of thinking and being no longer serve us, and yet the new path isn't yet clear.

During this phase, you might feel lost, confused, and even abandoned by Source, the spiritual guides or higher powers you once trusted. It's as though you're wandering through a dark forest with no map, no compass, and no clear sense of direction. It can be a deeply unsettling and painful experience.

Facing Our Shadow

What makes this phase so challenging is that it forces us

to confront our shadow selves. Those aspects of our personality that we've hidden, denied, or suppressed suddenly come to the surface, demanding our attention.

You may face fears, traumas, and unresolved issues from the past. It can feel like a battle with your inner demons. But remember, this struggle is an essential part of the healing process and you are indeed being guided at all times.

Embracing the Transformation

As difficult as the dark night may be, it's also a phase of profound transformation. Like the caterpillar in the cocoon, we must go through a process of disintegration before we can emerge as something new.

During this time, it's essential to be gentle with yourself, to seek support from trusted friends or spiritual guides, and to allow the process to unfold. You may find solace in meditation, journaling, or other spiritual practices that resonate with you.

The dark night is not a punishment but an invitation to a deeper understanding of yourself and the universe. It's a call to shed the old and embrace the new, to let go of what no longer serves you and open up to a higher level of consciousness.

Emerging into the light. Eventually, the dark night will pass, and a new dawn will break. You'll emerge from this phase with a deeper sense of purpose, a clearer vision of your path, and a greater connection to your authentic self. It may take time, patience, and diligent inner work, but the rewards are profound. You'll find yourself more aligned with your true nature, more compassionate, more loving, and more whole.

The dark night of the soul is not an easy journey, but it's a crucial one. It's a phase of inner alchemy, transforming the base metals of our being into spiritual gold. So if you find yourself in the midst of this dark night, know that you're not alone, and that this phase is temporary. Trust the process, embrace the transformation, and know that you are on a path to something beautiful and true. Remember, the darkest night will always give way to the light. In the deep and transformative shadows, we find the light of our true selves. Embrace the journey, for it is in these challenging moments that we grow, evolve, and truly become who we are meant to be. Here we should look to place the ego as the co-pilot and the soul on the driver seat.

The ßeta phase is the second phase of software testing that occurs after the alpha phase. During this phase, the software is released to a limited group of external testers or customers for testing and feedback. The focus of the ßeta phase is on gathering feedback from real-world users and addressing any issues that are found before the final release of the software.

This ßeta phase is the phase I am inviting you to create by taking your power back. The power to be your most authentic self. To be wild, creative, to open your heart, to remember we are all Gods and Goddesses having a human experience. To break free from any cages holding you back from stepping into your true potential. To be a Quantum Alchemist Master in your life and you will begin to see how you start to change the world but as the saying goes:

«The change starts with you.» - Unknown

To rebirth from the ashes like a phoenix and co-create with the universe from love and for love. Is fear holding back? What have you always wanted to do that you haven't done? What do you enjoy doing? What makes you laugh? What fills your heart? What fills your cup in overflow that you can then share with the world offering value and providing you with vision and purpose. Are you ready to change your codes, your software, your hardware? Are you ready to connect directly to your own Source of higher power? Whatever that is for you, it's simply perfect and beautiful.

I am not sure where I heard this exercise, so I give credit to whoever came up with this, but I will share it with you because I feel if you don't have a consistent meditation practice and are not in a place yet that when you quiet the outside and you are listening to guidance from a higher Source. This is a good exercise to start brainstorming and gaining clarity.

What are 3 things you love to do? What are 3 things the world needs right now according to you? What are 3 things you are good at? Taking all of the previous questions and answers into account, what are 3 things you can do that you can get paid for and are aligned with all previous mentioned?

The Deployment Phase: Once the software has been tested and any issues have been resolved, it is ready for deployment. This involves installing the software on the target system or environment.

Although we may have been deployed or we have been operating from a programming that has not been updated according to our own standards you can now build on your own ideas, use your own judgment, ask your own questions, re-write your own unique program become your 2.0 version or higher version of yourself, activate the unique DNA codes, light codes with the real code and information that is unique for you, make your own upgrades, get your own codes, all of that is inside of you. You have a unique way that you can help yourself and contribute to the world. Find your purpose, find your why? Find your vision? Remember the connection to your soul.

«God remains an illusion until you have realized him, and once you realize God, The world becomes an illusion.» - Unknown

In our quest to become the highest versions of ourselves, we are often faced with the challenge of transforming old systems and codes that have governed our lives. The process of rewriting these codes is both profound and deeply personal. It requires love, compassion, forgiveness, intention, and faith. The answers are hidden within your very being.

Love is the foundation of our existence, a divine connection that binds us all. To rewrite your inner codes, start by embracing love, not only for others but also for yourself. Recognize your divine worthiness and allow love to permeate every fiber of your being.

Compassion is the gentle hand that heals the scars of our past. Approach yourself with understanding, empathy, and kindness. Acknowledge your human frailties and recognize them as stepping stones on your spiritual path.

Forgiveness is the bridge that carries us from resentment to freedom. By forgiving ourselves and others, we break free from old chains and create space for new growth. Remember, forgiveness is a conscious choice, one that leads to a higher state of being.

Intention sets the direction of our journey. It's like setting a compass for our soul, guiding us toward our true purpose. Focus your thoughts and energy on what you truly desire and trust that your intention will lead you there.

Faith is the assurance in what we hope for, even when we cannot see it. Embrace faith as you embark on this transformative journey. Trust in the unseen forces of the universe, and have faith that you are guided and supported in every step.

The Maintenance Phase: The final phase of the software development process is maintenance. This includes ongoing support for the software, bug fixes, and updates to keep the software current with changing requirements or technology.

Regardless of the changes we make, we must upkeep the system mind, body, and spirit as one. Our ideas, views, perspectives on life and our belief system may change many times and we should be in a state of flow and open to holding many different possibilities for the expansion process to become easier for us. I am always growing, always learning, always a student of life, I keep asking questions and I will hopefully keep a curious mind as a child would, to be able to look at different ideas and perspectives and continue learning. I will use my previous life experiences as stepping stones for my next version. I will keep being patient, loving and forgiving to myself as I continue learning while trying to juggle and find balance in my life. Even though the pendulum may swing too much one way, I will remind myself to be aware of the zero point of coming back to being grounded and centered and start again as many times as necessary. I will auto correct the path or make a different path from love and peace that is more and more aligned with my soul and higher self.

In the dance of life, finding balance is key. Embrace the changes, learn from your experiences, and remain centered in love and peace. Your journey is a beautiful process of continuous evolution. Embrace it, and know that you are the creator, the developer, the programmer of your unique life and our collective experience.

CHAPTER 4
HOW THESE PHASES TRANSLATE INTO MY OWN PERSONAL JOURNEY

MY HERO'S JOURNEY

I was born in Pinar del Río, Cuba in this incarnation where mother nature reigns in all her glory. We didn't have much money, but I had a very happy childhood. We lived off of the land in a farm where I used to climb trees, play barefoot and be surrounded at any given time by over 20 animals and in my child's mind, I had everything I ever needed. Life was magical everywhere. It looked and it all seemed perfect from that little girl's perspective. I had a wild imagination and spoke with the trees and the animals as if it were something everyone should know how to do. I had the wildest dreams and would say it to my family and luckily, they respected most of my dreams, many prophetic in nature. Because many times I would say something and it would take place. They learned to make room for these dreams. They couldn't explain that there was some truth to it and it just became a thing around the house. There were several periods in Cuba where we went through a lot of struggles and even lack of food at the table, to the point where the family would take turns not to eat one of their meals so I could have it. On both sides of the family, as far back as both sides can remember, we come from a lot of poverty and lack where I would later in my journey learn where a lot of the limiting beliefs had been forming even before this incarnation.

My dad left when I was 2 years old to go to Miami, Florida in search of a better life. Not me knowing how much this what seemed like a small abandonment wound would affect me later on. I am not looking at it from a victim perspective. I understand today and we agreed on this for me to become who I am today. My father has been one of my greatest mentors and motivators in his own ways. We have both talked many times about this and have asked for forgiveness on both sides. I am sure there is plenty more to work on, learn, and growth we have left to do together. Without understanding why, as a child I told my mom I was moving to my neighbor's house to sleep there and move in with her. As crazy as it sounds, my neighbor at that time was much older than my mom. To me she was like a loving grandmother. She had already raised two children and two grandchildren of her own, so she had this beautiful motherly loving energy. I had no clue as a child what was happening to my mom when my dad left, but I couldn't feel that same amount of safety, security, love and nurture and emotional stability coming from her. Although today looking back, she gave me all the love she knew how to at the time and I was honored to have two mothers instead of one. As of the present moment my mother and I have done a lot of work together around these events and I am just thankful and honored her soul chose to endure so many things for me to have a better life then she did, understanding all the sacrifices she has made to push me forward and I also see how her mom did the same with her. We are all just doing the best we can with what we have. Now I see she was coping with the loss and being a single mom as best as she could. I made this transition and as time went by, I could see how I had developed these walls around love and connection so that I wouldn't be hurt or abandoned again. Of course, I wouldn't figure this out until much later on my hero's journey, but it partially originated here without counting past lives experiences, parallel lives, or future timeliness to make it less complex.

As time went by February of the year 2000 my mother and I traveled to Miami, Florida to reunite with my father. All of a sudden, one week before coming or so I found a baptism card that said my dad's name and another woman were a boy's parents. I had no idea about that situation until I saw the baptism card. I immediately asked my mother and she had no other option but to tell me not only that I had one brother but two from my father's side now. In my mind, my father still was this hero figure whom I highly regarded and this shredded that image into pieces as I understood my mother very deeply for the first time. I arrived to Miami, Florida in my teenage years without growing up with my dad and that transition was difficult because I didn't want him to tell me what to do and how to live, but I also was in a new country as a teenager that did not speak the language and needed help and guidance. I now understand my mother and father both did the best they knew how, they would even try to help me with homework and help me in the transition of acclimating to this new language and culture. It was a shock to me —this new reality— because I was used to being surrounded by people that loved me back in Cuba, and here I would wake up and be shipped in a bus to school and come home to find no one was home. My dad owned a cafeteria at the time and he and my mother were working most of the time and would get home around 11:00 pm. I wouldn't see anyone before going to bed or when I would wake up and much less, receive the kind of love I had back home. This did a lot of growing up for me pretty fast. I thought that I needed to be strong, independent and successful and for sure not trust anyone or fall in love or I would be let down or get hurt again. I had my first suicidal thoughts around this time and wrote a goodbye letter. Luckily, my dad found it and just out of shame that he had found it, I didn't go through with it and held on to fighting in this human journey.

I started working at the age of 14 since my mom knew someone that could get me a job and I asked herI wanted to do it. My plan was to leave home as soon as possible. Obviously, they did not know that part, but I was old enough to know that I wouldn't make it very far without money. I was not afraid of work as I used to work in the fields just for fun as a child. I enrolled in high school in a work program they had. All four years, I would be allowed to leave school early to go to work and it wasn't a lie: I was actually working. The more I worked, the more I saw the pay didn't match the work I did and the service I provided and that it wouldn't be enough to be on my own as soon as I thought. At the time I

started working, I was earning US$4.75. Then I got an incred-
ible raise to US$5.25. Can you believe it? I remember the
exact moment I opened the check to see my raise and I realized I needed to study to become «someone» to get out of
poverty. I was in a filing room carrying 30 lbs (13.6 kg) boxes
weighing 103 lbs (about 47 kg) at that time. That was
another pivotal moment. I left home shortly after (still in my
teens) and went to live with my first girlfriend. I left out the
small highlight: I am gay, yes. In pre-kindergarden, when I
was asked, I said:

«What do you mean boyfriend? I have a girlfriend.»

Well, since then it is still the same. I did at some point in
high school try different relationships with boys but the
chemistry just wasn't there.

I moved in to a US$400 a month efficiency with my girl-
friend at the time. We could barely afford it. I was at the
pawn shop every month seeing what I could pawn to make
the rent. We slept on a mattress on the floor and cooked
outside with a camping stove. Every time I was going to pay
with my card I was afraid it would decline and I was at a
negative balance in the bank many times. This motivated me
even more. I went to Miami Dade College and graduated. My
aunt mentioned I should go into Nursing. My first career
choice was to be an Archeologist, but the pay was not as high
as I wanted. Then I wanted to become a Psychologist, but I
was told that to earn the kind of money I wanted would take
at least 10 years of study. There was nothing else I liked and
throughout history, all women in my family have been heal-

ers, midwives, nurses, or doctors. So why not nursing? I had no idea at the time I could listen to my own intuition, higher self or my guides. So I was people-pleasing to some degree. I had no idea how to maintain boundaries, and I was looking for approval from any source since my parents said some very harsh things. I will leave out about me being gay and the way I would end up. Regardless of all the obstacles, I enrolled in nursing school. At the time I had like three part time jobs to make ends meet.

I had no idea that this is where I would be meeting my twin soul. We sat next to each other in nursing school. Her name is Ailýn. She was the angel God had sent to save me, because I was about to go through a very wrong path. That's what my cousin and others did because it paid more. I can genuinely say that love —the very thing I had been running away from— saved my life. I ended the previous relationship I had and the fact that Ailýn was married and with a 2 year old child did not make things any easier for us. I remember telling her I could step away because she could lose her family. I knew the pain that causes and from what she used to tell me how her family was so united and loving. She is such a brave soul and has such a big heart she did not care. Love was everything to us. She was kicked out of her house with her child sure enough, as I had warned. Her family took a while to come back around and we had to move in together. We lived in a small apartment on Flagler and we couldn't pay US$575 monthly rent. We had an efficiency and all of us slept in that same room together. I worked as a Home Health Aid taking care of older people: bathing them, cleaning their home and assisting them with anything they needed. I did that some time, since I was studying to become a nurse and needed income to pay the rent. Again love got us through until we graduated from the Practical Nurse. We started making US$15 an hour each and we thought we were millionaires from where we were before. Some of our happiest memories were around this time. We thought, hoped and dreamed that when we graduated, our lives and that of our family would drastically change for the better. Love got us through all the ups and downs and until we officially became Registered Nurses. At that time, we were able to move to a duplex with a yard for Daniel, our son, to play soccer (For most readers outside the United States, I mean what you know as football.), his favorite sport. We thought we should become Nurse Practitioners so we can buy a house and live better. Many more student loans later we became Nurse Practitioners. Again love got us through all the difficulties. Here, in this stage of the hero's journey, we were in what can be considered as The Ordinary World: This is the hero's everyday life and environment before the story begins. It's a safe, familiar world, but the hero feels restless, sensing that something is missing.

As time went on, we had enough money saved. All we have ever heard is that you should get married and buy a house, so as soon as they legalized gay marriage in Miami, Florida, we did and bought a house as well. We were living the dream. We had been together for 10 years at the time. We worked so much. We barely saw each other because now we earned more but we had more expenses. No one ever taught us about saving, investing, real estate or generational wealth. We had no point of reference to help and guide us; it was basically the blind leading the blind, as the saying goes. Little did I know that my spiritual awakening was beginning, my extended dark night of the soul was here to alchemize me and break down all the systems that were in place. Now that I had finished the top of my career and found out that the material things were not giving me the happiness they promised, I was extremely angry at God and started questioning God pretty intensely. I was like:

«I cannot believe this is the beep that you created. This is hell, not heaven.»

I created my own living hell to the point where I shut down my wife and my son. I lost track of what was important. I let myself be distracted by worldly illusions that promise happiness. I struggled with addiction and suicidal thoughts once again and it got to a point where I had no reason to get up in the morning. I was better off dead from my perspective at that time. I lost focus of the love I had for my wife and child. We decided to take some time apart to figure ourselves out. Here is where I received the call to adventure in my hero's journey: where the hero receives a challenge or invitation to embark on a journey. It's the inciting incident of the story, a problem or challenge that disrupts the ordinary world.

In 2022, I had a near death experience. I invited Ailýn to California. At the time she had also been working with my same teachers learning energy work, breathwork, Akashic Records and other modalities, of course each privately in our own separate sessions since 2018. I never heard anything from her private sessions and vice versa. She also decided to do the deep work. We were in a good place as friends and had figured out co-parenting by then. Our claires had been opening up slowly and we were able to access the Akashic Records, meditate, fasting, journal, tarot, breathwork, and some other forms of energy work. I felt called to go to this place and we decided to go camping and just talk more about where each of us was and go from there with no pressure and no expectations. It was a mission to get there. We had the fastest Uber drivers I've ever had and I wasn't sure if we would make it. We stopped at a Walmart nearby and bought our camping gear. We had originally planned to stay three days. However soon you will find out that changed pretty quickly.

There was a group camping on this site but when we arrived, we noticed there was a shed that was empty. We asked if we could sleep there and they said yes, that it wasn't being used. So, we said why not place all our stuff and went outside to enjoy the night sky. I noticed that this particular night was the darkest night I have ever seen but thought nothing else of it. We went to bed excited for the following day. At this time, I had been working on waking up gratefully in the morning but wasn't quite there. I felt like I was forcing myself to be grateful but did not feel that authentically, as I was going through so many life changes and wasn't sure where my life was going. I felt as if I was at a dead-end road type of situation. Back to this night, I remember at some point feeling very cold and then very hot like temperature changes but I did not wake to that feeling. I cannot pin point to why, when, how long it lasted, or how it happened but the experience to follow myself felt like a near death experience.

All of the sudden. I am conscious and awake outside on the camping ground and I start to see Egyptian heliographics appear in green, red, and gold colors like laser forms. Unexpectedly, I was sensitive and could perceive vibration, energy, and sacred geometry all around me. This place was covered by an electromagnetic field. I could see Nadis in the body. They showed up for me as green laser dots and lines. I felt as if time did not exist. Then something clicked and I thought:

«Oh my God. Did I die?»

And I heard a voice say «Yes». Immediately I was taken into a dark spiral of darkness, like this void vacuum-like feeling. I remember going through what seemed to me as different hells. I do not recall the exact number because it was very traumatic. I might have chosen to forget some of this to be able to cope with this event. So these hells were not one particular place. They were scenarios of all my fears. They were self-created hells looking back at it now. It seemed as if I was faced with all my fears and worse case scenarios with those fears. I remember a particular one was fear of clowns which in my regular human experience. I don't ever recall being afraid of that. Another was with a chainsaw and someone trying to kill me as well. I remember I could not cry, I remember freaking out because I couldn't feel my body and I didn't have my senses. One fear in particular that scenario was played over and over many times like a hell loop was the fear and guilt of dying. I remember saying but:

«Did I die? What about my mother, my wife, my child?»

It was all this guilt and sadness of how I could have done things better with them.

I remember questioning God if dying was this, then this was bullshit what he had created. I was very judgmental and said infinite profanities in Castilian (aka «Spanish») to God and his/her creations. Where was heaven while I was in what seemed like hell like scenarios? I thought I had been a good person. Looking back at this could also have to do with being raised Catholic and the belief of heaven and hell, but who knows. I was so tired after going through all these self-created hells and once I reached the acceptance of dying there was a turning point. Started what seemed like a life review but this review started from some time before incarnating. I saw my family on my father's side seated in a circle and the role they each played in my life and how we each choose to incarnate and help each other. Soul contracts we made with each other to help us in our process of evolution. I do not recall seeing my mother's side of the family at this point. I could see how I choose to incarnate, you already know your name, date of birth, you choose the place of birth and your parents, amongst other things.

I was then shown that I have been everything: all the elements, parasite, rock, tree, water, fire, earth. I could actually feel as if I was each element in experiential form and each has its own degree of consciousness. I have been from each continent, each race and skin color, feminine and masculine. I could see many past lives passing right before me at lighting speed but somehow, I could still differentiate and perceive each of those lives as different and what I felt with each. I have lived in other galaxies and planets, aside from the Earth, and I was shown just many lives that I could now maybe refer to as fractals of my soul. This went on until a point where I could feel ONENESS. I was ONE with the ALL.

I was then shown what I could describe in words as a domino trail of what my soul has lived with Ailýn, my twin soul. Most of the time, I was shown things that were very simple, me caressing her face, her arm, looking into her eyes. Going to sleep and waking up, like seeing the day to day of the relationship. I was able to meet my higher self. She comes across as a very wise medicine woman. I was also able to meet Ailýn's higher self; she comes across as an Asian Goddess.

I was then sitting at the center of the earth with mother nature across from me until I became one with her. Then I was sitting across from God and we could see the Earth turning at the speed of light with this electromagnetic field surrounding it. I remember asking God many existential questions including why the suffering, the sickness, poverty, about money and so on. Then the only thing I recall is he placed his hand on my shoulder in this particular case, I did see God as a male with short white beard in his late 60's because that is what my consciousness at this time could understand God as. Now —of course— I see God in every-thing and everyone and at that point immediately all my questions were answered and I had an understanding of why everything happens; how it happens, but I was not able to bring that back with me aside from having faith and trusting that it is all happening for our highest good. I was able to see my life passing before my eyes: past, present and future like a life review with much love and no judgment at all, in the process. Guilt and sadness dissipated and I just felt this warm loving energy and presence.

I remember being obsessed about finding the light, but not any light: I wanted the sun. Don't ask me why, I have no idea. «At some point I understood we are all ONE GOD/SOURCE, all fractals of the same Loving energy. I remember God saying God is within you and that the present moment is a gift, and he/she said something about the beautiful world we created together, that was the main idea that we created it together, co-creators with the Source. I finally became the sun and my chest exploded with light. I was the sun in sunrise and I was every ray of light. I just became energy and felt how this energy was supplying all that is, like life energy that runs through all life forms.

At some point, I came back to my body and woke up and it was as if I had literally been born again. I could see everything in micro details; I could enjoy everything using my senses and just everything was magical and perfect exactly as it was and the sun; I have never seen the sun this way. The light from the sun that morning has had no comparison. My love for Ailýn at this point was bigger than it has ever been. I explained the event to her and she fully supported me through grounding this process and integrating it. She has a very beautiful grounding, loving energy. She mentioned she spent all night in this black void. Every time she had any fearful or worrisome thought, a colorful spiral with a whooshing sound would appear, which to her meant that it didn't matter, so each of us went through a process in our own way, to be able to support each other on what was to come after. I finally was grateful to wake up each morning and feel it for real this time. To me, opening my eyes next to my loved ones and serving where God needs me and coming to terms with the present moment and acceptance of what is knowing is working for my highest good. I sometimes fall off the wagon and bicker with Source and my guides because things are not how I want them and when I want them to be but tend to go back to center pretty quickly.

Both of our claires continued opening at a much faster pace after this night. We decided to stay in California for a couple more days and give each other another chance from a different perspective. Love again had won this battle. I was once again exposed to death and rebirth, another ego, death, yet another episode of my extended dark knight of the soul. When we came back to Miami, we decided to move to a modest apartment in Westchester to be close to Ailýn's parents who were of an age that needed care as they had several falls, and her dad had a stroke around the same time and we were not able to buy a home at that time due to the high interest rates and prices. It was a time of starting over, of rediscovering who we were beneath life's layers, society, our ego construct, who we were as a couple and as individuals and everything else that had been added.

The extended dark night of the soul has continued being one of the most challenging phases of my life from 2018 until

2023. When I started this healing journey, I thought there will be a quick fix, one thing and done: I will be healed and forever happy. With time, I have understood that this is a spiral ever-changing, ever.evolving, always changing positions in the spiral and looking at things from a different place and unlearning, relearning and revisiting things you thought you learned. Cycles and moments, peaks and valleys. The more I learn, the more I understand there is to learn and even when you do, it's subject to change by the observer. I have learned to keep an open mind and not have attachment to any one particular idea or universal truth. This student mindset keeps my heart open to receiving and being shown new information and a new perspective. We are all students and teachers of each other. What is different now is the tools I have to navigate the ups and downs and challenges and come back to center to the zero point to the observer of my human experience. The open heart to enjoy the present moment and to look at things not as good or bad but as an experience and a learning opportunity that holds within a gift a lesson for my greater good and all of those involved in it.

Although I had heard the calling as part of my hero's journey, I went through a phase of refusing the call: despite the allure of the adventure, the hero might initially refuse or hesitate to embark on the journey due to fear, duty, or any form of insecurity. In this case healthcare, which had been my anchor, I always loved caring for people and seeing them improve their health and go back to enjoying a healthy life with their loved ones, the underlying why of being of service was still there but the profession no longer resonated with my evolving self, since it was taking a lot of time away from my family and my priorities changed. I wanted to do something more aligned with these new priorities. After owning a medical spa business that I ended up selling, I ventured into the dynamic world of real estate, hoping to find my place to learn about real estate, generational wealth and investing. But the call of my soul was too strong to ignore, although I was being of service in a different way and did have more free time to focus on my family, the universe, in its infinite wisdom, was guiding me towards my true purpose. Although I had a lot of remembrance and guidance at this time about my soul mission, I sure was lacking the resources to complete it and I was venturing into different things with the hopes to make enough income to complete this.

As part of the hero's journey meeting with the mentor: where the hero encounters a mentor figure who provides guidance, wisdom, and often a special tool or knowledge that will be needed later. This mentor prepares the hero for the challenges ahead. In my case I have not only had the honor of having physical teachers but also the help from my guides, Source and other plant allies that continued presenting themselves to me when needed. I had many mentors and guides along the way and hope to have many more. Some of the plant allies were Ajo Sacha, Lupuna, Mama honguitos, abuelo fuego, Ayahuasca, and many others. Some of my greatest teachers have been plants, Angels, Archangels, the 13 rays, Ascended Masters, Krishna, Shiva, Shakti, Buddha, Lao Tzu, our start brothers and sisters and many more. As I am non-religious, I can learn from different masters using my own discernment and take what serves me and leave the rest. I have also had the honor of working with many wonderful shaman's, medicine women, Akashic Records teacher, energy and light workers, psychologist and psychiatrists, and many more but there hasn't been one particular mentor always there guiding or teaching me and I believe this has been perfect for my own journey as it has provided such a wide perspective and flexibility in learning.

«I looked in temples, churches, & mosques. But I found the Divine within my heart.»-Rumi.

So, I left real estate and embarked on the most fulfilling journey of all, starting my soul-aligned business Quantum Alchemist Master where we empower you to become your own master by looking within. This is where I share all our tools: Akashic Records & Awakening Course, our Day Challenge, Connecting with your higher self, guides, and Source from within, Breathwork, guided meditations and many tools for exploring yourself by looking within, Awakening, Alchemy, and other courses to help you navigate through this journey where you are your own master, guide and guru. We just accompany and guide you in the remembrance and alchemical process so you don't have to do it alone. You will find we created a supporting community with step-by-step guidance to assist you in the awakening and ascension process we created all we wish we had when we were going through that process ourselves. We still continue, since it's an ever-evolving process.

One of the most difficult things in the process was

speaking my truth and authenticity in any form. Written, video, art forms, live events. I noticed looking back that I was more afraid of my light, of my gifts, of my most authentic expression, of my own greatness. Why was that? What were the underlying subconscious beliefs sustaining remaining stagnant and unseen. I looked in past lives, parallel lives and my current life. There were many lives where I had been killed for speaking my truth. Subconsciously I was running the programming that once I had success, I would lose friends and family and people will see me differently. I had doubts about my ego and my humility and how I would integrate the change, and so on. The more I looked under the rug the more dirt I found. I was always a quick warrior to go through my own darkness and the abyss with a blazing rainbow sword protected by my guides but why was I not as courageous and as determined to step into my true potential into my own light. So, little by little I worked out these learning opportunities from the eyes of love, patience and compassion for myself in my human journey. I am doing the best I can and just bringing awareness, this can be a great first step shedding a light of any size in a room full of darkness is a beacon of hope.

I remember when I recorded the first set of videos, I wanted to share with the world through my Instagram page. I immediately got really sick right after and decided to push back the release of these videos. Similar events and push backs have happened with my poems, my books, and anything that would involve being seen, speaking my truth, and sharing my perspective. Through the use of many tools, I mention throughout the book including but not limited to breathwork, meditation, art, qigong, yoga, NLP, Hypnosis, Energy Healing, Akashic Records, Plant Medicine, and others. I was able to overcome and integrate the changes, align more with my higher self, Source within me, my mission and purpose and truly embody that which I am now, this ever-changing version of me in this particular timeline. You have the power to change to take response-ability for your life, your choices, your habits, your reactions, and so on. I am just one of many examples. If I can, anyone can. Believe me and if you don't believe me why don't you try it? You have nothing to lose. If you don't change, nothing changes, but for you to change, it has to come from you. With your awareness and willingness, you can ask for the necessary support and guidance throughout your journey as I have many times but all should lead you right back to yourself. Go within, don't be afraid of what you will find light and darkness, feminine and masculine and everything else in between. Embrace the journey within to find the jewel in the lotus and the path to higher consciousness and love for self and others.

«I have been the seeker and still am, but I stopped asking the books and the stars. I started listening to the teaching of my soul.» - Rumi

This is where the next step of the hero journey comes in crossing the threshold: where the hero commits to the adventure and leaves the ordinary world behind, entering a new, unfamiliar realm. This is the point of no return. A testament to the resilience of the human spirit, the power of transformation, and the magic that happens when we align with our true purpose. Creating this soul-aligned business, we encountered much resistance as we live in perceived duality. The trademark process was a nightmare, not to mention the cost of it. They kept asking for more money and more money. Every time we heard back, they wanted something new approved. As I am not a trademark attorney and I was trusting one, I was naïve in the process and probably overpaid and got ourselves into major debt as we did not have the money at the time to do the trademark, but listening to my guides I did it anyways. I trust there is a divine plan and the universe is guiding and supporting me in this process.

What I am about to share with you now is something I deeply meditated on if I should share it or not, as it is a very personal and difficult process but after much thought, I figured it could serve someone if they too are going through it to know that you are not alone. It is about my Kundalini awakening process. This happened during the eclipse on October 14, 2023. I meditated for about 3 hours during the eclipse with a specific grid I was guided to create using Lemurian crystals from Minas Gerais, Brasil. Previous to this, I had been meditating with these crystals and knew they were very powerful. I will not go into the details of the meditation, but I did receive many light codes and information as well as seeing a golden serpent rising from under the ocean on the earth, traveling through the tallest mountains and then into my body and rising throughout my body. I had received instructions a year before to prepare my body for a big change during this eclipse, but I did not listen. I had not changed my eating habits as cleanly as I could have, nor did I exercise as much as I should have. The compound effect of all this and my extended dark night of the soul process after 5 years all led to my Kundalini awakening. I did not feel much at first, but by the afternoon that day I had collapsed. I completely stopped eating, my body started shaking arms and legs, shivering throughout the body, heart palpitations, and my stomach was feeling very energetic. I figured this would pass if I went to bed. I could barely sleep and had temperature changes between cold and sweats, palpitation and body movements strange to me even coming from a healthcare background. They seemed like movements you would have when having seizures but I was conscious and alert while they were happening. These kept happening for about three weeks at random times throughout the day. I would later come to know these movements as Kriyas. I will sum up this process, but it was very scary, sad, and uncertain because I did not know what was happening. Very quickly my body became very weak, and my mental health was facing a crisis it had never encountered before. I did not feel safe in my mind, body, or spirit. I could only take in fluids and puree foods for 21 days after this event and lost a total of 18 lbs (about 8 kg). I was hospitalized 2 times without any positive findings. All tests, lab work, diagnostic imaging, everything came back normal. There were no explanations for these symptoms. I thought I was dying of an unknown cause. I wrote a goodbye letter to my family and a beautiful poem to my wife. I asked my spiritual teachers and they were not sure what was happening as I had omitted the meditation I had done and what I saw we were looking for physical illnesses. Please do not assume if you have my same symptoms that you should not get checked by a healthcare professional. I always recommend ruling out any underlying condition causing your symptoms. By the end of 21 days, I learned to listen to my body. Never before could I listen to my body. I could literally just know clearly what I could eat and what I couldn't, what energy the food I was eating had and became very sensitive to all energy from people and places. During this process, I had amazing support from my wife, my son, my parents, mentors, and loved ones. Everyone pitched in somehow to help me get through this, I am forever grateful I could not go through my journey without all your love and support.

This was yet another death and rebirth process that I could not see at the time. I have learned countless lessons from this event in my life as well as from all others. When I was starting to recover, I remember thinking I am going to create a program that can help people going through difficult process, crisis, suicide, addiction, mental health, not feeling safe, and others not as a stand-alone or as a treatment but just as another optional tool and I will make it available for free, and so the 7-Day Challenge was born, currently there is a paid version, a free 14 day free trial which gives you access for free and a free 1 Day sample. Once I overcome and alchemize this cycle in my life. I understood it was happening for my highest good and that of the whole. I was being shown everything, that I could no longer sustain, everything was collapsing to begin anew. I opted to take responsibility for how I reacted and alchemized this experience rather than being a victim of the circumstance, what this is trying to teach me, and how I can transform it and use it for my highest good and that of the whole. I invite you to take responsibility for your life; look at this from a different perspective. Mind, Body and Spirit aligned and integrated with a different understanding. Some of my biggest teachers now were silence, breathing, the space between the space, the arts, simplicity, surrender, non-attachment, no rush, no destination, no carrot to chase, gratitude, presence, the eternal now moment knowing for certain that no matter how it may seem all is happening for my highest good and that of the whole. Once again, I had died and was born again and I created after this process a FREE 14 day trial of our 7-Day Challenge available to all those who need the support going through a difficult cycle in their lives. I would love your support by sharing it with someone that can benefit from this and if possible, bring this program to addiction, rehab, prisons, mental health, corporate spaces, athletes, and other spaces for really anyone who may need it, it is available for free to help all those who resonate with it. You can find this on my Instagram @quantumalchemistmaster and on our website quantumalchemistmaster.com.

«When the faith is strong enough, it is sufficient just to be. It is a journey towards simplicity, towards quietness, towards a kind of joy that is not in time. It's a journey that has taken us from primary identification with our body and our psyche to an identification with God, and ultimately beyond identification.» - Ram Dass

At this point I am writing this book. I am halfway through my hero's journey and that is what I can share with you, as I am sure there will be many more books to come where you can follow more as the journey unfolds in divine timing. As you delve into these pages, know that this is not just my story. It's a reflection of the universal journey we all undertake, the quest for meaning, love, purpose, the search for our soul, Source and some of the biggest life burning questions. I don't offer you one universal truth or answer. I share with you my journey and my ever-changing perspective. Through the highs and lows, the joys and sorrows, remember that every experience is a stepping stone, leading us closer to our true selves. We are learning, alchemizing, and evolving together as a whole. Please know you are not alone and you are loved and guided always.

CHAPTER 5

BREAKING THE CAGE

YOU HAVE THE POWER

A cage made out of scarcity, fear and limiting beliefs, thoughts and actions keeping us small and following the crowd.

«There is nothing more confirming than the prison we don't know we are in.» - Shakespeare

These fears, limiting beliefs, scarcity being passed down generation after generation deep into our DNA and belief system. Giving our power away to external «gurus», «governments», «leaders» and «masters»? What if each of you are your own master? What if all the answers lie within? What if you are a God ora Goddess with infinite potential? What if society has created a rat-race full of external distractions, so you don't remember your true divine nature and come full force into your power. Society is no other than ourselves less conscious, less aware, with more greed with other goals, not necessarily aligned or operating from love and in service to oneness further away from the original Source of LOVE that we inherently are.

A course in miracles says:

«Spirit is in a state of grace forever. Your reality is only spirit. Therefore, you are in a state of grace forever.»

What if they are using the media, food, water, school systems, music, movies, contaminating the environment and everything they can. To keep humanity in lack, in fear, in suffering, sickness and separation. When I refer to «they», «them», «society», «the elite», «the external world», «the matrix», I am referring to a part of us less conscious that because of this is leading the collective consciousness and therefore our collective reality. However, the collective reality is essentially the sum of all parts meaning the sum of all the individual consciousness. We are the «matrix». We are «they». We reinforce the beliefs imposed unto us by the outside world and we do the same with our children. Remember they can't violate your free will but what they can do is condition and reinforce a set of beliefs that you can believe to be true and you will reinforce that on your own thinking it's the best for you. For example, and I don't want to make this book about that,but it is worth mentioning. With the COVID vaccine we all had a choice, but the mass media supported it, all the way from presidents to artists to everyone else supporting it. That influenced our decision, thinking it was safe to get the vaccine. Some workplaces like mine at the time and my wife's made it mandatory to get the vaccine to continue to have a job. Meanwhile the big pharma and the elites keep profiting from experimenting with human life, making everything harmful from the water we drink, to the food we eat to the products we use in our household daily. All I am saying is we need to take a closer look at our programming both from the external world and our internal world once you do that you are better equipped to make better choices.

«The world will ask you who you are, and if you do not know, the world will tell you.» - Carl Jung.

We buy into the fear, into the lack, we put ourselves in the hamster wheel. Our thoughts, emotions and beliefs create our reality. The real war is fought going within and by not participating in the system as much as possible. Freedom is our birthright. Let's reclaim our birthright, let's stop giving our power away. Allow your old self to die and be reborn as the phoenix rising and taking flight. In my opinion we need 8 billion leaders to come into their own inner power, find their own voice, their own calling, remember who they truly are and why they are here. Stop giving your power away; find your own truth. Our challenges may be just here for us to overcome them, remember that we are co-creators and find solutions that we are not yet aware of. We are eternal souls, infinite beings, living in an infinite universe, with infinite possibilities, with infinite dimensions and time past, present and future all co-existing simultane-ously. You are everything and everything is you. We are the universe and the universe is us we are the container and the container is us and we are ONE.

Stop holding back your dreams, your desires, your magic, your voice, your truth, your purpose, your vision. Stop letting others dim your light. You are all sovereign, powerful, worthy and love. Believe it we all are. The heart knows what the mind and eyes cannot see. There has been research about that. Your intuition knows. You know deep down inside you hold the key; you are the fifth element; you are the master and the hero you have been waiting for; you are the ONE. We all are, there is no separation, only the illusion of it. In Quantum physics it is well known that the observer creates the reality so are you willing to see yourself differently from the eyes of LOVE of divinity of the sovereign and powerful being that you are?

A course in miracles says:

«You respond to what you perceive, and as you perceive so shall you behave. The Golden Rule asks you to do unto others as you would have them do unto you. This means that the perception of both must be accurate. The Golden Rule is the rule for appropriate behavior. You cannot behave appropriately unless you perceive correctly. Since you and your neighbor are equal members of one family, as you perceive both so you will do to both. You should look out from the perception of your own holiness to the holiness of others. Miracles arise from a mind that is ready for them.»

Let's rewrite our story together. We are transitioning into

the great awakening. If we are a fractal of Source and Source is within us and around us how could we allow anything other than LOVE to win. Other than joy, happiness, and abundance. So those of us less conscious, the work is done from within. We are our most important project. We are the creators of our individual and collective reality. So what are we waiting for? We have help from the multiverse and all of our brothers and sisters who are awakening alongside us. We are loved and guided in every moment; we are never alone. Even if some cannot see it, hear it, smell it, even if you cannot use your senses to know this or even if your psychic abilities are not fully developed yet. It's like a dog whistle most humans cannot hear it but dogs can, something similar just because you cannot perceive it with your senses it does not mean it does not exist. Our species is evolving past our 5 senses.

How long are you willing to feed into this story and to pass this down to your children and your children's children? Are you ready to tap into your soul, into your own sacred connection to Source and all that is. Are you ready to quiet the outside noise and listen for the next steps in your journey? Are you ready to activate your unique gifts and start sharing it with the world? Are you ready to remember your mission, your purpose, your vision? Who are you really and what did you come to do to planet Earth?

So, I ask you: If there were nothing stopping you, no fears, if you had infinite abundance and unlimited resources, what would you do? What are your dreams? How are you doing what is aligned with your heart and soul? How are you living in alignment with your purpose?

Despite your current life circumstances could you take a leap of faith and do it anyways? Are we going to keep diving into the working hard, grind and burn out routines that are affecting ourselves, our family, our mental health and just our overall health? We need to find balance, we need to create a new way of living and experiencing life to be of freedom and abundance for all just like earth has seasons and cycles.

Follow your heart, follow what gives you joy and happiness. Fear, anxiety, stress, and being overworked for how long can you sustain that and if so, what will your quality of life be? Are you going to keep following the dangling carrot? Or are you ready to listen to your heart, to your soul, to your higher self, to Source and the masters within you?

Open the door to your heart, you had the key in your pocket all along. Once you come in, tune with your heart's desire. There is a specific message, gift, codes, energy, blueprint and so much more that you came to share with the world. Once you tune into that you can share from a place of authenticity without seeking outside for validation or feeling worthy you are already whole, you are already enough but when was the last time you listened to your heart? Have you found meaning and purpose in your life that lights up your soul when you wake up in the morning? Ask yourself questions until you find that and follow the breadcrumbs in that direction.

«Be yourself. Everyone else is already taken.» Oscar Wilde

Many beings in the multiverse are here volunteering to

help in the awakening and ascension process. However, I don't necessarily agree with the terms ascension because it also may imply some form of separation. I believe this is just a natural cycle of our collective species and if you want to think of ascend, I would say then this is done by subtraction of everything you think you are that you are not by infinite death and rebirth cycles.

«The soul does not grow by addition but by subtraction.» - Meister Eckhart

Many volunteers came to assist, each with their own unique path, message, mission, and purpose to assist us all as a collective as ONE.

You are waking up; you are remembering; the masks are falling off. The system is collapsing and can no longer sustain the illusion, the cage is breaking, and each of us is breaking free and empowering the rest to do the same. I encourage you to stop trying to fit in but rather embrace your uniqueness, your gifts. If you don't fit in maybe you are here to create something new from your perspective.

Maybe just maybe you are more than the famous black sheep. Maybe you are a multicolor rainbow, multi-dimensional, godhead, divine, infinite sheep, so how can that be put in a cage in a set of rules about how and when you should live your life and create? Let's all take our power back and create the world we all deserve, to leave this world better than when we found it. The elite group that run's society can no longer keep up with the amount of us awakening and sharing our truth with the rest of the world. We are using the same systems they created to advocate, to fight back, to gain our freedom, our power back. The power goes back to the people and the new earth is already a reality.

The time is now to start asking questions and arriving at your own conclusions, keeping an open mind to an ever-changing perspective. I invite you to look at some of the free resources I offer and use your discernment for whatever resonates as truth for you. I invite you to search for The Volunteers Telepathic Version, The Gateway experience done by the CIA, Near death experiences on YouTube. There is so much information not being disclosed. Sacred texts burned, altered, classified information. They don't want you to remember your divinity so you can keep playing the game but you my dear reader can change everything in it, starting from within. This is what you would call an inside job.

The universe acts as a hologram, a change. One of us also affects the rest. Like a broken mirror with many pieces one reflection is still reflected in the other pieces. Separation is an illusion for division and control of the masses. At any time, we can tap into the collective consciousness, the collective universal knowledge, Source, the collective heart and start creating from love and for love. Let's pulse together with one heartbeat, one world, one universe, one mind, one earth, one multiverse. The more we seek to know thyself, the closer we get to the Source, to unity to oneness. So if you are going to start anywhere, start from your inside world and eventually that will be reflected as your outside world.

«As above, so below, as within, so without, as the universe, so the soul» - Hermes Trismegistus

Let's dream together. Let's co-create and if we had infinite potential and possibilities (as we do), what could we create? If we had unlimited resources and nothing stopping us, how big would we dream? What would we dream into reality? What is your vision as we step into the golden age, an age of peace, love, abundance, prosperity, co-creation, collaboration, love, acceptance, unity, oneness? If we all create the golden age individually and that is how is reflective for the collective, how will you design and create your golden age?

Hidden truths will be revealed. We the people will step back into our own power, into our own coronation as Gods and Goddesses of this universe and co-creators.

«The Goddess is not separate from the world- She IS the world, and all things in it; Moon, sun, earth, star, stone, seed, flowing river, wind, wave, leaf and branch, bud and blossom, fang and claw, women and men.» - Starhawk

All it takes is for you to believe in yourself, know that is possible and know yourself to explore yourself and the infinite possibilities and power that you have within you. Explore your infinite divine multi dimensionality. We were born for this, this is part of our purpose to create a new world to collapse the illusion, the fears, the limitations. We are infinite unlimited all-powerful beings fully connected with the divine, Source, sacred knowledge, quantum field we are here to bring the remembering of heaven on earth, to bring Christ consciousness to the masses the return is within.

You deserve the love, the joy, the abundance, the forgiveness, the amazing sacred sex. You deserve to live freely and fully to embody all of your vastness and share your unique imprint with the universe. Let go of fear, limitations and any limiting beliefs, nothing can be taken away from you as you are everything, you are already whole, but do you believe that? If not yet, look within, the answers are within you. We are transitioning from living in fear to living from and with love. From lack to abundance. From grind and over work to flow, easy, joy, creation, and sharing your gifts with the world. (We all have them, seriously.) You just haven't stopped the outside distractions and looked within and stopped to listen. Let's do a massive detox. I was like that too. From seeking outside for validation to inner wisdom and intuition.

The universe is always supporting us and life is happening for us so if we have full support. So, it all comes down to faith and trust. Are you willing to take the leap of faith knowing that you will be supported? Are you ready to live a life of magic and miracles? How will you write, edit, and produce the script of your very own fairytale? Will your fairytale include dragons, fairies, mermaids, or more? The keys to the kingdom citing the Bible here Matthew 18:1-35:

«Truly, I say to you, unless you turn and become like children, you will never enter the kingdom of heaven. Whoever humbles like this child is the greatest in the kingdom of heaven.»

LIKE PABLO PICASSO SAID:

«Anything you can imagine is real.»

So, if the imagination is one of the keys, what will you imagine?

CHAPTER 6
A DIFFERENT KIND OF ANATOMY
LOOKING AT OUR BODY FROM
A DIFFERENT PERSPECTIVE

I wish I could have learned a different perspective about anatomy in school. In a spiritual perspective, the anatomy of the human body is often seen as more than just a physical structure. It is believed to be intertwined with various spiritual elements that contribute to a person's overall well-being.

I am not an expert at anything but I would love to suggest we include a more holistic approach in school's curriculums. Maybe add:

- Mindfulness, biodiversity and sustainability courses to the curriculum.
- Add yoga, breathwork, meditations, and ways in which to regulate the nervous system.
- Add more collaborations and in class projects not sent home.

- Add more creativity, critical thinking, and problem solving.
- Add more creative and art projects of different kinds.
- Add gardening and grounding time.
- Add good eating habits and optimal physical health.
- On higher grades add financial literacy with real life scenarios.
- On the science/health side let's include a more holistic approach, herbal medicine, natural remedies, changing the first line of treatment to natural resources before using a drug to treat it right off the bat. etc.

Starting in public schools. I assume private schools have a stronger curriculum, but if they don't already include this, I highly suggest it.

Physical Body: The physical body is the tangible, material aspect of a person. It includes organs, tissues, bones, and all the physical systems that allow the body to function.

Energy Body: Many spiritual traditions describe an energy body that exists alongside the physical body. It is believed to consist of various energy centers, such as chakras or meridians, through which life force or vital energy flows. Practices such as energy healing aim to balance and optimize the energy body.

Chakras: Chakras are energy centers or vortexes that are believed to exist within the subtle energy body. These centers are thought to correspond to different aspects of a person's physical, emotional, and spiritual well-being. There are many but seven main chakras are associated with specific qualities and are often represented as spinning wheels of energy along the spine.

Meridians: Meridians are channels or pathways through which vital energy, often referred to as Qi or Prana, is believed to flow. These channels are associated with traditional Chinese medicine and are thought to influence the overall balance and well-being of the body and mind. Acupuncture and acupressure techniques aim to stimulate and balance the flow of energy within the meridians.

Higher Bodies: Some spiritual systems propose the existence of higher bodies beyond the physical and energy bodies. These may include the mental body, emotional body, causal body, and spiritual body. These bodies are believed to correspond to different levels of consciousness, awareness, and spiritual development.

Spiritual Centers: In addition to chakras, some spiritual traditions recognize other spiritual centers or points within the body. These may include the third eye (located in the forehead between the eyebrows), the heart center, or the crown center (at the top of the head). These centers are often associated with expanded consciousness, intuition, and spiritual connection.

Mind and Consciousness:

I believe there exists a profound distinction between the mind and consciousness. This distinction is one of the keys to unlocking the doors to a different understanding. The mind, being the thoughts, emotions, and memories. It is the repository of our fears, desires, past experiences, and more.

The mind is a ceaseless chatterbox, constantly dancing to the tune of external influences and internal turmoil. It is the stage where the dramas of ego identity and unfold, where judgments are cast, and where the noise of the world finds its echo.

Consciousness, on the other hand, is the silent observer, the eternal witness to the mind's turbulent antics. It is the vast, unchanging awareness that resides deep within us, beyond the fluctuations of time and space. Consciousness is the pure, unadulterated essence of our being, untouched by the stains of conditioning and worldly attachments. It is the Source of our inner peace, wisdom, and connection to the divine.

Imagine, if you will, that the mind is like a stormy sea, with waves of thoughts crashing upon its surface. Consciousness, then, is the serene depth of the ocean, where the turbulence of the mind cannot reach. It is in this stillness that we discover our true nature, our oneness with all of creation.

Embark on the journey within and self-inquiry. Through any of the tools I have mentioned before or those that resonate with you such as: breathwork, meditation, art, nature, alone time, outside world distraction detox, sense deprivation, plant medicine, and much more we learn to quiet the mind's incessant chatter, creating space for the light of consciousness to shine forth. Self-inquiry, on the other hand, allows us to question the nature of our thoughts and beliefs, our programming leading us to the realization that we are not the mind, but the consciousness that observes it.

In this journey of self-discovery, we come to understand that the mind is a tool, a vessel through which we navigate the material world. It is a gift, but also a challenge. When we mistake ourselves for the mind, we become entangled in its dramas and limitations. But when we recognize our true identity as consciousness and loving awareness, we transcend the limitations of the mind and step into the boundless being that we are into experiencing a different kind of peace, joy, grace, and freedom. The mind is but a passing cloud in the vast sky of consciousness. Embrace the stillness within, and you shall find the peace, love, and wisdom that have always resided in the depths of your being. I hope some of this serves as a guide towards the realization of your true self.

«My brain is a receiver, in the Universe there is a core from which we obtain knowledge, strength, and inspiration. I have not penetrated the secrets of this core, but I know it exists.» - Nikola Tesla

- Soul or Spirit: Spirituality often acknowledges the existence of a non-physical aspect of human beings, sometimes referred to as the soul or spirit. It is seen as the eternal, divine essence that transcends the physical body. The soul is often associated with qualities such as consciousness, awareness, and interconnectedness with a higher power or universal consciousness.
- Energetic Aura: The aura is considered a subtle energetic field that surrounds and permeates the

physical body. It is believed to contain information about a person's emotional, mental, and spiritual state. Some spiritual practices focus on cleansing, balancing, and protecting the aura to promote well-being.

- Elemental and Cosmic Connection: There is an emphasis on the connection between the human body and the elements of nature or cosmic forces. These elements can include earth, air, fire, water, and ether (or spirit). It is believed that harmonizing with these elements can support spiritual growth and well-being. In spirituality, the comparison between minerals in the human body and the universe is often made to explore the interconnectedness and unity of all things.

- Like the Microcosm and Macrocosm: The belief is that the human body reflects the universe on a smaller scale. It is seen as a microcosm, embodying the same elemental composition and patterns found in the larger macrocosm. The minerals present in the body are seen as a reflection of the minerals and elements found in the broader universe.

The concept of the seven stages of consciousness, for all I know there could be infinite stages of consciousness. I am using 7 for simplicity and to be able to understand the main idea. This is just one interpretation of seven stages of consciousness.

1. Physical Consciousness: This is the most basic level of consciousness, associated with awareness of the physical world and our sensory experiences. It includes our perception of the external environment through our senses.

2. Egoic Consciousness: At this stage, individuals develop a sense of self or ego. They identify with their thoughts, emotions, and personal history. Egoic consciousness can lead to attachment, desires, and a strong sense of "I" and "mine."

3. Intellectual Consciousness: This stage involves the development of rational thinking and intellectual abilities. Individuals begin to question and analyze their experiences, seeking knowledge and understanding. It is a stage of increased self-awareness.

4. Psychic Consciousness: Psychic consciousness is associated with intuition, heightened sensitivity, and the ability to perceive subtle energies and information beyond the physical senses. It often involves experiences such as intuition, telepathy, and extrasensory perception (ESP).

5. Spiritual Consciousness: This stage represents a shift towards a deeper spiritual awareness. Individuals begin to recognize their interconnectedness with all of existence and may experience moments of profound insight, unity, and transcendence. It is a stage of awakening to spiritual truths.

6. Cosmic Consciousness: At this level, individuals experience a profound connection with the universe or cosmos. They may have a sense of unity with the entire universe and a deep understanding of the interconnectedness of all things. It is often associated with a sense of oneness.

7. Divine Consciousness: Represents a complete merging with the divine or ultimate reality. It is a state of absolute oneness, bliss, and liberation from pain and suffering. In some traditions, it is seen as a state of union with God or the Source of all existence.

Iᴛ's important to note that these stages are not necessarily linear, and individuals may experience them in different ways or at different times in their spiritual journey. There is no one-size-fits-all model. The concept of stages of consciousness can be very complex but I hope with this it kind of gives you an overall idea.

The perspective and imagination exercise I will mention here will trigger some people to stop reading the book right away as they may not share this view. This is especially true if you come from a science, very religious, very logical or black and white way of thinking and/or operating which by the way is beautiful and perfect for you in your journey, and I have been there as well. All is always in perfect harmony and exactly as it should be. If you use logic as the guiding force for discernment like I once was very set in stone on my world view at one point in time. I respect your decision as a sovereign being, but I definitely invite you to be flexible, have fun with it and continue to listen not to agree to disagree but to take with you the main message that is in this book to empower you to step into your own power into your own truth not to believe mine, to find freedom, sovereignty and Source within yourself, each in its own unique way. Take everything you come across lightly and use discernment and intuition your inner compass to guide you in what is useful for you.

For a moment, if possible, I invite you to think of «now» for instance one big body of light with no name, no face, no religion, no sex, just light, love, energy, contraction and expansion, cycles, feminine and masculine, the full spectrum of light, also having chakra systems and consciousness floating in the middle of what could be perceived as a black void, silence and nothingness, all and nothing at the same time, form and formless, visible and invisible, as if Source were the center of a blackhole. Using thought, intention, imagination, energy, vibration, frequency, sacred geometry, and electricity, chaos moves in perfect harmony and LOVE as the life force that creates and lives through everything that exists through every fractal of creation. It meditates in an eternal dream that births infinity and all of creation including physical matter. There are infinite dimensions, universes and worlds within this body of eternal light and darkness. Each world within a spiral form made up of a double helix DNA that eventually transforms into a triple helix DNA and all the elements in the universe, containing the same life force, chakras and energy fields as the one unified field. Now let's zoom out more. You can also see different layers and energy surrounding the body in rainbow colors just like we have the etheric body and the 7 bodies that surround our physical body. You continue to zoom out and now you are looking at the void with the luminous body and surrounding energy in the middle of the void. Outside of this, there is an invisible electromagnetic field. When you zoom into this it seems like atoms that vibrate and have electricity and communicate with the entire field in perfect unison. I would like for you to imagine for a moment Source as one big unified field or a cell with 2 nucleolus or a cell in the telophase where the cell is not fully divided into individual cells, if you want to hold this, but imagine it contains both masculine and feminine structures being one infinite cell that holds all life forms, the multiverse and all of existence, right before it separates into 2 independent cells all coming from the one parent cell in this case Source/God. So now you have a double cell structure holding all life forms and multiverses surrounding these two cells. You see the infinity symbol in rainbow rays and the infinity symbol is not static but energy in motion.

«Your vision will become clear only when you look inside your heart; who looks outside dreams; who looks inside awakens.» – C.G.Jung

Now from this macro perspective. Let's zoom into the human body and the physical experience as a micro perspective of the whole ecosystem. If you think for a moment our body is being guided by a higher intelligence, our atoms, our cells, our organs, it's an organized chaos that works in perfect harmony to animate our life in the worlds of forms. We have constant death and rebirth processes working for our highest good that allows for life to continue. This perceived chaos is perfectly synchronized for optimal survival of the organism and the species.

With this perspective, if we hurt another, we are only hurting ourselves. If we only think about individuality, about our own species, essentially, we are the whole fragmented, the many forms and planes of existence. So how can we co-exist in more harmony in more love, with more awareness and respect for each others as equals, as teachers and students with equal weight and value, regardless of sex, ethnicity, or anything else that may cause division. How can we put all of our differences aside and start placing all the different perspectives together to have a better under-standing of the great mystery from this plane of existence and this level of consciousness? Although I may not fully understand it and will be a student of the great mystery, I may not have the full perspective of Source or of my higher self. Here we may very well use what we have been shown, gifted and share it with each other. Let's work together in collaboration. Let's use all the clues from the past and the present to build the rainbow bridge of love and unite heaven and earth and reclaim the LOVE that we ALL are.

This book is non-dogmatic. However, I do like to include quotes from different sources that may relate to a specific point I like to share.

The idea is that we have been created in the «image or «likeness» of God. I like to refer to human beings having certain attributes that reflect aspects of God's nature, like our ability to reason, to love, to feel, to communicate, to make choices, co-create, etc. I also like the idea that everything and everyone is inherently worthy, has value, deserves respect and care and that we are all fractals of the divine. This helps us look more within for love, for compassion and a deeper understanding of ourselves and our relationship to one another and to Source regardless of what that looks like for you, regardless of the name, the face, the sex you assign to it. For those that have had a near death experience and have encountered God. It may show up a little differently for each person in a way they can feel safe, familiar, loved, guided and comprehend and accept God due to much separation and religion. God/Source may be different for so many.

«I am nothing. I'll never be anything. I couldn't want to be something. Apart from that, I have in me all the dreams in the world.» *The Book of Disquiet* by Fernando Pessoa

CHAPTER 7
THE HEART AND THE BRAIN
THE TWO AS ONE

Most of our lives we are taught to use our left side of the brain, our logical, analytical aspects. In school we are guided to strengthen and use our left side of the brain like a muscle. While one is strengthening, the other one is wasting away by not using enough of the right side of the brain.

The heart and the right brain are like special gateways that can help us connect with our intuition, higher wisdom, and our true selves. Let me explain their roles to you:

The Heart: Our heart is more than just a physical organ; it's also a center of energy and the Source of emotions, love, and compassion. In many spiritual traditions, the heart is associated with qualities like intuition, empathy, and spiritual connection. When we focus on our heart, we can access a deeper understanding within ourselves, connect with our higher self, and feel a connection to something greater, like the divine or the universe.

To tap into the power of the heart, we can try practices like heart-centered meditation or simply being aware of our heart space. By directing our attention and intention to our heart, we can experience a greater sense of harmony, alignment, and connection with ourselves, others, and the world around us.

The Right Brain: Our brain has two halves, and the right hemisphere is known for its creative, intuitive, and holistic thinking. Some people call it the «intuitive mind» or the «creative mind». The right brain is believed to help us connect with our subconscious, where our intuition and higher guidance reside.

To awaken our right brain, we can engage in activities that stimulate creativity, like art, music, visualization, meditation, breathwork or exploring our dreams. By quieting our analytical mind and allowing our intuitive side to come forward, we can gain valuable insights, inspiration, and a deeper understanding of our life's purpose and journey. Both the heart and the right brain act as channels that allow us to access higher levels of awareness, connect with our authentic selves, and tap into universal wisdom. By practicing activities that activate and align these aspects of ourselves, we can experience a stronger inner guidance, expanded awareness, and a deeper connection to our Source of inspiration.

The truth you seek is not in this book, is not in my opinion or the opinion of others. The truth and wisdom you seek is inside of you. This comes from alignment with yourself as Source as all there is as I AM that I AM and I AM and I create. The more you practice quieting the outside noises the more you will learn to listen and access the knowledge within. In my path asking questions, slowing down, cultivating self-love, self-awareness, self-forgiveness, journaling, gratefulness, breathwork, accessing and working with my Akashic Records, meditation, plant medicine, alchemy, painting, singing, dancing, being more in nature, tuning into my heart, listening to my intuition, got me to this understanding.

The outside distractions are there as distortions of reality, go deep within and find your true magnificence. Be aware of your thoughts, feelings, patterns, actions, and anything stopping you from reaching your true potential. Be so quiet until you reach peace, until you reach zero point, where the illusion of separation banishes away and you have certainty and clarity of who you are. You are so grounded, so unshakable that there is no going back.

Once you reach oneness, the void and the quantum field of infinite creation and possibilities you become more present in the now and you choose your truth, your reality, what and how you want to experience it. Remember you always have free will and this cannot be violated. So, I ask you what will you choose? Once you reach this point you become a vessel for the universe to work for and through you for your highest good and all of those involved in it. We are much more capable than we have been led to believe our soul is an unstoppable force of love, creation and an extension of Source itself.

«My ally is the Force, and a powerful ally, it is. Life creates it, makes it grow. It's energy surrounds us, and binds us. Luminous beings are we, not this crude matter. You must feel the force around you; here, between you, me, the tree, the rock, everywhere, yes.» - Master Yoda

FINDING YOUR MISSION, purpose, and divine plan is a deeply personal and spiritual journey. It involves seeking a deeper understanding of yourself, connecting with your inner wisdom, and aligning with your spiritual beliefs. While the specific process may vary for each individual, here are some general insights and steps that can help in discovering your mission and purpose in a spiritual context:

Self-Reflection: Take time for introspection and self-reflection. Explore your passions, values, and interests. Reflect on the experiences and activities that bring you joy, fulfillment, and a sense of meaning.

Inner Listening: Cultivate a practice of quieting the mind, such as meditation or prayer, breathwork, darkness retreat, mantras, learn to access and work with your own akashic records to connect with your inner guidance and intuition. Listen to the whispers of your heart and the nudges of your soul. Pay attention to the messages and synchronicities that arise in your life.

Alignment with Values: Identify your core values and examine whether your current life and activities align with them. Clarify what matters most to you and explore how you can infuse those values into your daily life.

Service and Contribution: Consider how you can use your unique skills, talents, and interests to make a positive impact on others and the world. Explore ways in which you can contribute your gifts in meaningful ways that align with your spiritual beliefs and values.

Seeking Guidance: Seek guidance from trusted spiritual mentors, teachers, or advisors who can provide support and insights on your journey. They may offer perspectives, tools, or practices to help you navigate and discover your mission and purpose but remember they don't have the answers, YOU DO!

Surrender and Trust: Recognize that your mission and purpose may unfold gradually and evolve over time. Practice surrendering to the divine flow and trusting that the right opportunities and experiences will present themselves when you are ready.

Intuitive Action: Take inspired and aligned action toward your mission and purpose. Follow your intuition and inner guidance as you make choices and decisions that align with your values and contribute to your sense of purpose.

Gratitude and Celebration: Cultivate an attitude of gratitude for the journey itself and celebrate your progress along the way. Acknowledge and appreciate the steps you are taking towards living your mission and purpose.

Remember, finding your mission, purpose, and divine plan is not a destination but a continuous exploration and growth process. Stay open to the unfolding of your path, trust your inner wisdom, and embrace the unique journey that is meant for you.

From the knowing that you are a fractal of Source, Source incarnates experiencing itself through you, having a human experience in a continuous path of expansion. From that point of origin, you are already mastery, love and everything you seek outside is inside of you. Simply being alive is enough. You don't necessarily need a complicated mission. Each mission is unique for each and all equally important.

Regardless, you will know when you know it is deep and clear and no doubt will exist. Meanwhile be patient, be forgiving with yourself, simply by being in this present moment you are enough, you are in the right place and time for your highest good even though it may not look that way when you are in what seems to be a storm. There is a gift in the challenge, there is a lesson, there is a purpose. Do you trust? Do you believe? Do you have faith? Start by loving yourself and looking within and it will all start making sense in divine timing when you are ready.

You have no idea how many times I used to talk to Source and say:

«Now I am ready. Now anytime is as good as today. Try me now. Give me the money now, the freedom, etc. Again, seeking Source as outside of me, when we must go within. When you look back in retrospect you will see why it had to be that way.»

The art of aligning our senses with the heart is crucial to assist us in navigating our spirit-human journey. We've been conditioned to process everything predominantly with our minds. The mind, with its analytical prowess, often takes the lead. But there's a deeper, more profound way of experiencing life, and that is through the eyes, ears, touch, taste, and scent of the heart.

Seeing from the Heart

When you look at the world with your physical eyes, you perceive shapes, colors, and movements. But seeing with the heart? It's like uncovering hidden layers of a painting. The heart sees emotions, intentions, and the unspoken symphony of life. A sunset becomes not just a visual treat but a soulful embrace of the universe.

Hearing from the Heart

The heart listens to the melodies that go beyond words. When someone speaks, the heart hears the undertones of their emotions, their unvoiced hopes, and silent fears. It's an attuned ear to the harmonies of the universe, the whispering trees, and the symphony of waves.

Smelling from the Heart:

With every inhale, the heart can pick up the subtle fragrances of memories, emotions, and feelings. It's more than just identifying a scent; it's about connecting deeply with the stories and moments that a particular aroma evokes.

Tasting from the Heart:

To taste from the heart is to savor life in its entirety. Every morsel becomes a tale of the earth, of the hands that crafted it, and of love. Food isn't just nourishment for the body; it's a celebration for the soul.

Touching from the Heart

Our skin is a wondrous organ, sensitive to the slightest of breezes and the gentlest of touches. But when the heart gets involved, every touch becomes a language. A handshake transforms into a connection, a hug into a profound exchange of energies.

Now, you might wonder: how do we shift from sensing with our minds to sensing with our hearts? The magic lies in mindfulness and intention. Before you see, take a moment to breathe and ask, «What does my heart see?» Before you listen, quiet your mind and tune into your heart's frequency. With each sense, consciously redirect your focus from the head to the heart.

Embracing life through the heart's senses opens up a world rich with deeper connections, more profound insights, and a symphony of emotions. It's a journey of authenticity, of truly diving deep into the myriad experiences that life offers.

As you traverse your unique path, I invite you to pause, feel, and let your heart lead the way. It's a dance of senses, and the heart is an ever-willing, ever-passionate dance partner.

CHAPTER 8
MASCULINE AND FEMININE UNION BALANCE
THE COHESION PROCESS

The sacred dances of Shiva and Shakti, Isis and Osiris, and the Yin and Yang, are a reminder of our life journey.

Shiva and Shakti: The Cosmic Dance In the rich traditions of Hinduism, we encounter Shiva and Shakti, the divine masculine and feminine energies. Picture Shiva, the still, transcendent consciousness, and Shakti, the vibrant creative force. Their union creates all existence, a dance of life that vibrates through us all.

Isis and Osiris: Love and Rebirth In the fertile lands of ancient Egypt, the love between Isis and Osiris became a legend. Osiris, embodying fertility and life, was tragically murdered, and his loving wife, Isis, the symbol of wisdom and motherhood, resurrected him. Their story is a beautiful reminder of love and life's cycles. Their union represents the balance and harmony of complementary forces.

Yin and Yang: Harmony in duality in Chinese philosophy, the Yin and Yang gracefully encapsulate the balance of existence. Yin's gentle receptiveness complements Yang's assertive activity. Together, they flow in harmonious unity, a symbol of how contrasting forces can coexist and create beauty.

These symbols are more than ancient concepts. They mirror the balance and unity that we can find within ourselves and in our relationships with others.

Humans as the Godheads

We must also embrace the divine spark within us. This is not a claim of supreme power but an acknowledgment of our potential to connect with the divine essence that resides in each of us as fractals of the divine.

Many mystical traditions teach that we are one with the divine. This is not mere poetry but a profound perspective we can awaken to if we so chose, all paths are perfect. Co-creators with the Divine: We are partners in creation, able to shape our reality and manifest our desires. Aligning with the divine will allows us to transform ourselves and the world around us.

Reclaiming our power, now is the time to remember our divine nature, to rise above the illusions that have long held humanity captive. The power of love, light and consciousness is within us, not in the hands of a select few.

You are perfect just as you are as a spark of the divine, capable and worthy of love and abundance. Let us recognize our divine essence and cast aside the veils of forgetfulness. As we raise our consciousness together, we embrace the freedom and joy that is our birthright.

I invite you to question and reflect on the teachings shared in this book. May they guide you on your path to self-discovery, inner harmony, and a deeper connection with the universe.

CHAPTER 9

LAWS OF THE UNIVERSE
A BASIC GUIDE TO THE HUMAN JOURNEY

Our vibration and consciously aligning it with our desires and intentions, can help us utilize the Law of Resonance to create a life filled with joy, fulfillment, and purpose. As we embark on this spiritual journey together, I invite you to explore these profound laws that govern our universe. They are the whispers of wisdom that guide us to live in harmony, love, and understanding. Here, in this sacred space of insight, let's dive into the essence of these spiritual laws and the teachings of the Law of One, embracing them as guiding lights on our path to higher consciousness.

Embracing the Spiritual Laws: A Guide to Vibrating in Loving Order with the Universe.

The universe sings a harmonious melody, a song of unity and connection. We are all notes in this grand symphony, resonating and vibrating in accordance with universal laws that guide our lives. These laws, though invisible to the physical eye, are the spiritual fabric that weaves our existence.

The Law of Divine Unity

Everything in the universe is connected. You, me, the trees, the stars; we are all expressions of the same divine energy, dancing to the same cosmic rhythm.

The Law of Vibration

We are energy, and we approach others and our experiences through vibration or resonance. Aligning with love and positive intentions allows us to connect deeply with life.

The Law of Correspondence

«As above, so below; as inside, so outside.» The macrocosm reflects the microcosm, guiding us to understand that our inner world shapes our outer experiences.

The Law of Attraction

What resonates with you, comes to you. Attract love, joy, and abundance by cultivating these vibrations within.

The Law of Inspired Action

Connected to attraction, inspired action urges us to take steps aligned with our deepest desires.

The Law of Perpetual Transmutation of Energy

Energy never dies; it transforms. Embrace change as a natural part of the universal dance.

The Law of Cause and Effect

Every action corresponds to a reaction. Mindfulness in our choices leads to harmony in our lives.

The Law of Compensation

We get what we give. Let love, kindness, and compassion be your gifts to the world.

The Law of Relativity

Everything is relative, dependent on perspective. Embrace neutrality, understanding that all is part of the divine order.

The Law of Polarity

Balance in all things. Recognize the opposites and find harmony in their dance.

The Law of Rhythm

Life is a cycle, a rhythm. Flow with the seasons of life, growing and evolving.

The Law of Gender

Embrace the masculine and feminine energies within, seeking their balance and unity.

Embracing the Law of One

The Law of One is a spiritual philosophy that unifies the above laws and takes us deeper into the understanding of our oneness with the universe. Through many teachings we learn of the infinite creator, the nature of reality, and our evolutionary journey through consciousness. This philosophy encourages us to serve others, exercise free will responsibly, and continually evolve towards love and understanding.

Living the Law of Resonance

Similar to the Law of Attraction, the Law of Resonance teaches that our energies attract similar energies. Your thoughts, emotions, beliefs, and actions resonate, attracting experiences and relationships that reflect your vibration. Conscious awareness and intention in your energetic state can lead you to a fulfilling, harmonious life.

The Law of Impermanence

Teaches us that everything in this world is in a constant state of change. Just as the seasons shift and the tides ebb and flow, so too do our lives and experiences. Embracing this truth allows us to release attachments to the past and worries about the future, fostering a deeper appreciation for the present moment. By understanding impermanence, we can find inner peace and wisdom, knowing that every emotion and experience in life are impermanent, and it is in embracing this impermanence that we truly learn to live in harmony with the ever-changing universe.

These spiritual laws are not rules or commands but rather a gentle guidance that leads us towards a life of purpose, joy, and connection. Understanding and living in alignment with these laws enables us to vibrate in loving order with the universe, reflecting the divine unity that we all are. In our daily lives, let us take inspired actions that resonate with our true selves, serve others with compassion, with healthy boundaries and recognize the interconnected dance of all existence. May our journey be blessed with wisdom, love, and the beautiful music of the universe. Embrace these laws, for they are the keys to unlocking a life of profound spiritual growth and fulfillment. May we walk this path together, vibrating in harmony with the loving embrace of all that is and our interconnectedness.

CHAPTER 10
PROPHECIES
WHAT I WAS TOLD

I received prophecies from my guides that I would like to share with you in this book. I would also love to invite Earth and wisdom keepers from all parts of the world to come together and write another book with the different information and prophecies given to us for the new earth, so it does not only have to belong to a few but make it available to ALL as ONE.

I would like to invite conscious leaders of the world to write a multi-author book.

Possible title of this book:

THE BLUE BUTTERFLY MISSION: Building The Rainbow Bridge

IF IT RESONATES WITH YOU, you have been receiving synchronicities just with the information on the title alone pointing to this and if you haven't noticed that yet, I always invite you to consult within, meditate and see where it leads to. I would love to get together and see how we can birth this mission together. If someone reads this book and this calling resonates, I would love to receive your help and input in making this happen, you can reach me on instagram @quantumalchemistmaster or via the contact page at QuantumAlchemistNow.com

This mission has come about many, many times in many forms. However, there is a particular meditation insight I would like to share here with you. I connected to Source through my heart, I can see mother earth inside the core of the earth and mother earth and I are standing at the peak of this beautiful rainbow mountain and there is the biggest abyss you can see from the tip of the mountain and she says to me: «Take a step» and I said: «I will die, there is nowhere to step on to.» he gave me a soft smile and she repeated: «Take a step. I will walk with you. You are not alone.» As I took the first step, a rainbow bridge of light began to form with every step and she said to me: «With every step you take closer to your soul's mission you will be helping to build the rainbow bridge.» Then she said to me: «Take a seat,» and again with my doubt and judgment, I said: «There is nowhere to sit,» to which she gave me another soft smile and repeated the same. I took a seat and sure enough I was held, sustained, provided for, even when I thought it was impossible the rainbow bridge continued to appear and sustain me. As I was sitting there with Mother Earth, a blue butterfly came and landed on my left hand and it was a great lesson, one of many I have received from the spirit realm. It is with the greatest honor, humility and responsibility that I accept and embody this mission. If you feel called to join me and contribute in any way, please let's talk, we have amazing and joyful work to do.

Now I will share with you some of the prophecies that have been shared with me by my guides. I also sometimes receive the prophecies and I am not entirely sure what it means but I will share it anyways with an open heart and maybe it resonates with someone who has been given more information about these and we can piece it together and learn more together as the great mystery unfolds itself in the eternal now.

Prophecy 1

«The red and blue dragons will unite to form the rainbow serpent.»

Prophecy 2

«There is the possibility of a war that will want to use nuclear weapons and this will be very detrimental to humanity.»

I was guided to write this book and request a 10-year peace treaty among all nations to help prevent this from happening.

PROPHECY 3

«The white dragon warrior will unite the 7 heavens.»

As we walk together on this incredible path of spiritual evolution, we come across the concept of the seven heavens, a notion embraced by many traditions across the world. These seven realms represent various stages of consciousness or spiritual dimensions, each holding unique qualities and lessons. Together, we'll explore this profound concept and the practice of unifying these seven realms, a journey towards our true Self.

THE SEVEN HEAVENS - A Map of Consciousness

Physical Realm: This is the domain of our body and the tangible world around us. Here we learn to connect and honor the physical existence.

Astral Realm: Venture with me into the world of dreams, emotions, and subconscious where the ethereal meets the tangible.

Mental Realm: We'll explore the space of thoughts, ideas, and concepts, where the mind's landscape expands infinitely.

Causal Realm: This realm speaks of cause and effect, intentions, and actions. Here we understand that every choice carries a consequence.

Spiritual Realm: It is where we connect with the divine and realize the spiritual essence within and around us.

Divine Realm: This is the level of pure consciousness and

divine energy, where separation dissolves, and we embrace oneness.

Absolute Realm: The ultimate destination, beyond all form, where we merge into the infinite essence of consciousness.

UNITING the Seven Heavens - The Path Within

Uniting these seven heavens is an inner pilgrimage. It's a transcendental process, leading beyond our physical limitations to higher levels of awareness. Through practices like meditation, breathwork, prayer, or shamanic journeying, and others we find the stillness to look within. Together, we'll navigate through these realms, finding new depths of self-discovery and transformation. We'll unveil the interconnectedness of all existence and the magnificent unity in creation.

Tools for Our Journey

Embarking on this path requires patience, dedication, and the right tools. Here are some that have served me on my journey:

Meditation: Our key to inner stillness and awareness.

Breathwork: Techniques like shamanic, holotropic and other breathwork practices guide us in navigating deeper into our inner world.

Shamanic Journeying: Explore other realms through drumming and repetitive sounds.

Yoga: Cultivate inner peace and divine connection through body, breath, and mind.

Plant Medicine: A respectful approach to powerful allies

like ayahuasca, peyote and others can deepen our insights. Seek guidance from experienced practitioners when working with plant medicine.

Silence retreats, darkness, sense deprivation

- Nature immersion.
- Prayer
- Art/Creativity
- Many other forms

Uniting the seven heavens is a profound journey of self-realization and transformation. The tools and practices we've explored are gateways into this wondrous path. Approach each step with love, respect, and an open heart. Let experienced guides accompany you in the remembrance but as tools or mirrors to remind you to look within, the mastery is within you. For this journey is not just about reaching a destination; it's about realizing that we are, in essence, the very path we tread.

Prophecy 4

«The white wolf will lead the Americas.» - *Cosmic Consciousness*

PROPHECY 5

«When the eagle and the condor fly together, we will rise again.» - *Cosmic Consciousness*

There is already an existing Eagle and Condor Prophecy this is just how I received it.

PROPHECY 6

«The blue butterfly mission & the green dragon prophecy will happen simultaneously, helping humanity in the process of evolution.» - *Cosmic Consciousness*

Here is another prophecy not provided by my guides, but that has had a great impact on my journey and I wish to share it with you all:

A prophecy that extends its radiant arms to embrace not only the ailing Earth but the very core of our beings. The Rainbow Warrior Prophecy, as it has come to be known, is an ancient Native American teaching that has echoed through generations. It's a call to each one of us, a call to action, a call to become the warriors of the rainbow.

The prophecy tells us of a time, perhaps the time we find ourselves in right now, when the Earth would be in turmoil. A time when the natural balance would be disrupted, and a new tribe of people, known as the Rainbow Warriors, would arise to heal and restore.

· · ·

THE EARTH IN CRISIS: Understanding the challenges we face today.

The Emergence of the Rainbow Warriors: Recognizing the innate warrior within us.

The Role of Spirituality: Connecting with the Earth through our spiritual essence.

Embodying the Rainbow Warrior Spirit: Living the teachings every day.

Healing the Self: The importance of personal healing on our journey.

Healing the Earth: How we can contribute to global healing.

The Power of Community: Coming together to effect change.

Activism and Advocacy: Raising our voices for what we believe in.

Creating a Sustainable Future: Making conscious choices for a better tomorrow.

Honoring Indigenous Wisdom: Respecting and learning from the wisdom of the first peoples.

The Interconnectedness of All Things: Embracing the unity of all life.

Mindfulness and Gratitude: Cultivating awareness and appreciation in our daily lives.

Overcoming Adversity: The resilience that defines the Rainbow Warriors.

Living the Rainbow Warrior Prophecy: Practical guidance for embodying the prophecy.

The Rainbow Warrior Prophecy is more than a tale from the past; it is a living guide that speaks to each one of us. It reminds us that we are warriors, equipped with love, wisdom, and determination to heal and transform.

This book is not merely words on a page. It is an invitation to embark on a journey of discovery, empowerment, and purpose. Whether you are new to this prophecy or have been walking this path for years, the insights and guidance within these pages are here to support you.

Together, let's become the Rainbow Warriors. Let's heal ourselves, heal the Earth, and weave a tapestry of hope, love, and harmony. The time has come to answer the call and co-create a new earth.

HERMES the green emerald tablet

As we continue our spiritual exploration, I wanted to mention Hermes Trismegistus and the sacred teachings encapsulated in the Emerald Tablet. Your heart may already resonate with these ancient wisdoms; perhaps you've even caught a glimpse of them in a dream or meditation.

Hermes Trismegistus stands as a beacon of wisdom. He is one of the many giants I stand upon to bring forth this book. Often identified with the Greek God Hermes and the Egyptian God Thoth, Hermes Trismegistus transcends cultural boundaries, representing the synthesis of Greek and Egyptian spiritual traditions.

This great sage is known as «thrice-great» due to his mastery over three realms: alchemy, astrology, and theurgy. His teachings have inspired countless seekers, philosophers, and mystics throughout history including myself.

The Emerald Tablet is one of the most revered texts

attributed to Hermes Trismegistus. This concise yet profound piece of writing is often seen as a cornerstone of Hermetic philosophy and alchemical wisdom. The tablet's thirteen lines are shrouded in mystery and metaphor, revealing timeless principles that guide us on our spiritual journey. Let's explore some of its central teachings:

The Principle of Correspondence: «As above, so below; as below, so above.» This axiom reminds us that everything in the universe is interconnected. The macrocosm is reflected in the microcosm, and by understanding one, we can understand the other.

The Principle of Transformation: The Emerald Tablet speaks of the transformation of the One Thing, symbolizing the eternal process of creation and dissolution in the universe. This teaches us the art of spiritual alchemy, where we transmute our base desires into spiritual gold.

The Unity of All Things: At its core, the tablet conveys the unity and interconnectedness of all existence. It speaks of a primal substance from which all things emanate, calling us to recognize our inherent oneness with all creation.

Embarking on the path of Hermes is to embrace a life of inner exploration and transformation. The teachings of the Emerald Tablet are not just historical curiosities; they are living principles that can guide our daily lives.

The wisdom of Hermes and the Emerald Tablet is a gift that transcends time and culture. Its teachings are as relevant today as they were thousands of years ago. May this serve as a guide on your spiritual journey, illuminating the path to inner wisdom and universal love.

CHAPTER II

CHRIST CONSCIOUSNESS

THE SECOND COMING OF JESUS CHRIST

A s we continue this journey together, let me invite you into looking at Christ consciousness from another angle or perspective as within oneself. If possible, don't dismiss the entire book just because you may not agree with this, there is much more on here than just this, take what serves you and keep moving. This journey transcends religious boundaries, and it is open to all who yearn for a deeper connection with the Divine.

«Use your own light and return to the Source of light. This is called practicing eternity.» - Laozi

The Christ Consciousness

What do I mean by Christ consciousness? It's a state of consciousness where love, wisdom, compassion, and unity prevail. It's the realization that we are all interconnected, and the awakening to the divine essence within us. Christ consciousness is not confined to one religion or belief system; it is a universal love that can be accessed by anyone willing to open their heart.

Finding Christ Consciousness Within

Understanding your divine nature: Recognize that you are a divine being having a human experience. You carry the spark of the divine within you, just as Jesus did. Embrace your true nature and let go of limiting beliefs.

Love and compassion: Jesus taught love and compassion for all. Strive to embody these qualities in your daily life. See others not as separate but as extensions of yourself. Love unconditionally, as Jesus loved.

Meditation and prayer: Create a sacred space within you through regular meditation and prayer. Connect with the Divine within, seeking guidance, and allowing yourself to be led by a higher wisdom.

Service to others: Through selfless service, you can experience the joy and fulfillment that comes from aligning with Christ consciousness.

Living Mindfully: Embrace the present moment, for it is where the divine resides. Be mindful in your actions and thoughts, and you will find that Christ consciousness is not a distant reality but a present truth.

Don't hesitate to seek the guidance of spiritual teachers or mentors who resonate with you. They can offer insights and practices that can support your personal journey however, that knowledge you seek is already inside of you.

Finding Christ consciousness within oneself is a beautiful journey of self-discovery, growth, and transformation. It's about embracing the divine within you and allowing it to guide your life. Remember, this path is not about conforming to a specific set of beliefs but about discovering a universal love that resides within us all. It's a journey that requires patience, dedication, humility, and an open heart.

In the words of Jesus:

«The kingdom of God is within you. May you discover that kingdom, the Christ consciousness, within your own heart, and may it illuminate your path».

I thought this would be a good place to speak about the process the ego goes through, and of course this can vary, but it can be tricky to decipher sometimes between thinking you are actually Christ, The Buddha, or another in your spiritual journey from the ego and the self. I respect all, I am no one to say you are not. I simply ask you to question everything all the time, even what you think you know, or who you think you are.

The ego can change as one progresses on the spiritual journey and here are some examples.

Ego Traps: Ego traps are processes that individuals can encounter as they explore their spiritual path. These traps often revolve around a sense of self-importance or superiority that arises from spiritual practices and beliefs. Here are some common ego traps to be aware of:

Spiritual Materialism: This occurs when someone believes they are more spiritual because of the external practices or possessions they have, such as practicing yoga, being vegan, or owning crystals. The focus shifts from inner growth to outer appearances.

Self-Righteousness: Feeling morally superior to others because of one's spiritual practices or beliefs can create a sense of self-righteousness. This judgmental attitude can lead to a lack of empathy and compassion for those who follow different paths.

Judgment and Condemnation: The ego can trick individuals into passing judgment on others who don't align with their spiritual values. This judgment can create divisions and hinder genuine spiritual growth.

Feeling of Superiority: The ego may lead individuals to believe they are more enlightened or spiritually advanced than others. This feeling of superiority can alienate them from those who are at different stages of their journey.

The Ego's Evolution on the Spiritual Path: As one progresses on their spiritual journey, the ego can undergo transformations. Initially, the ego might identify with the physical self and worldly desires. However, with spiritual growth, it may take on a different form:

Spiritual Ego: This phase occurs when individuals begin to identify with their spiritual achievements, practices, or experiences. They may feel special or «chosen» due to their insights or spiritual connections.

Transcendent Ego: In this phase, individuals might experience a sense of unity and transcendence, believing they have risen above their ego. However, this can lead to a subtle sense of separation, as they feel different from those who have not had the same experiences.

Integrated Ego: True spiritual growth involves integrating the ego rather than eliminating it. The integrated ego recognizes that it's a part of the self, but it doesn't dominate or distort one's perception of reality. It serves as a tool for navigating the physical world.

Becoming Aware of and Integrating the Ego: To become aware of the ego and integrate it in a healthy way:

Self-Reflection: Regularly reflect on your thoughts, emotions, and actions. Be honest with yourself about any signs of ego-driven behavior or attitudes.

Mindfulness: Practice mindfulness to observe your thoughts and emotions without attachment or judgment. This helps you catch ego-driven reactions in real-time.

Humility: Cultivate humility by acknowledging that you are on a journey like everyone else, and you don't have all the answers.

Compassion: Show compassion and understanding toward others who may not share your beliefs or practices. Remember that everyone is on their unique path.

Service and Contribution: Focus on how you can use your spiritual insights and growth to serve others and contribute positively to the world.

Seek Guidance: Connect with a spiritual mentor or teacher who can provide guidance and keep you accountable on your journey if needed.

Regular Self-Inquiry: Continuously question your beliefs, motives, and behaviors to ensure they align with your true spiritual values.

By becoming aware of ego traps, recognizing the evolution of the ego on the spiritual path, and integrating it into your daily life with humility and compassion, you can navigate your spiritual journey more authentically and without causing harm or distortions in your relationships and experiences.

A course in miracles says:

«Whatever is true is eternal, and cannot change or be changed. Spirit is therefore unalterable because it is already perfect, but the mind can elect what it chooses to serve.»

Finding the library within yourself

While the physical Library of Alexandria, The Golden Library or The Halls of Amneti may no longer exist in physical form, its legacy can be seen as a symbol of the pursuit of knowledge and wisdom. The idea of finding all of these within yourself refers to the concept that within each individual lies a vast reservoir of potential insight, and wisdom.

Here are some ways you can explore and tap into the sacred knowledge within yourself:

Self-Reflection and Inner Exploration: Engage in self-reflection practices such as meditation, journaling, or introspection to delve into your inner world. Set aside quiet moments to connect with your thoughts, emotions, and intuition. Quiet the outside distractions whether it be going to a darkness, silent, or plant medicine retreat or any other form of looking within. This process allows you to access your own inner library of experiences, insights, and wisdom.

Cultivate Awareness and Mindfulness: Develop a state of present-moment awareness in your daily life. Pay attention to the subtleties of your thoughts, feelings, and sensations. By being fully present, you can uncover deeper layers of understanding and tap into your intuitive knowing.

Connect with Intuition: Practice connecting with your intuition, which is the innate wisdom within you. Intuition can guide you toward insights, solutions, and ideas that may not be readily apparent through logical thinking alone. Trust your gut feelings, listen to your inner voice, and allow your intuition to guide you on your path.

Seek Knowledge and Learn: Engage in continuous learning and personal growth. Explore topics that intrigue you, read books, attend workshops, and engage in conversations with others who share similar interests. By expanding your knowledge, you broaden the range of insights and ideas that can emerge from within.

Embrace Creativity and Imagination: Engage in creative activities such as writing, art, music, or any form of self-expression that resonates with you. Creativity stimulates your imagination and allows you to access deeper layers of your consciousness, where new ideas and perspectives can emerge.

Trust yourself: Develop self-trust and confidence in your own wisdom. Recognize that you possess unique perspectives, experiences, and insights that can contribute to your understanding of the world and your spiritual journey. Trusting yourself allows you to access the sacred knowledge within.

Practice Self-Compassion, patience and self-love: Be kind and compassionate toward yourself as you explore your inner library. Embrace your strengths and accept all of you. Treat yourself with love and respect, creating a safe space for personal exploration and growth.

Remember, the process of finding the library of knowledge within yourself is a personal journey that requires patience, self-reflection, and an open mind and an open heart. Embrace your inner wisdom and trust that the answers you seek are within you, waiting to be discovered or remembered and shared with the world.

CHAPTER 12

DIMENSIONS

TRANSCENDING THE 3-DIMENSIONAL WORLD VIEW

When I speak of dimensions, I invite you to join me on a journey through different levels of consciousness, each filled with unique attributes, characteristics and beings co-existing amongst one another, not necessarily one higher or better than the other, simply different. To me, these realms aren't confined by numbers or rigid orders; they co-exist simultaneously, flow seamlessly into each other, representing profound levels of consciousness which we can access and navigate.

In our spiritual quest, let's strive to unite rather than divide, embracing various perspectives and respecting each other's views. This path is about creating a better reality for ourselves and for everyone around us, not about being right or wrong.

You may share a story similar to mine; I've wandered through countless books, seeking answers, only to discover that the wisdom from each has compounded into where I am today. There's no final destination, only continued growth and openness to different views and ideas. We may even find ourselves challenging our own thoughts, reshaping and expanding our understanding of reality. One day, we'll realize that the answers we seek are already within us, meanwhile let's use all available tools and resources to help us look within.

Let's take a gentle stroll through a different perspective of dimensions. In my opinion there are infinite dimensions and levels of awareness that exist simultaneously, but I will mention some aspects to bring forth some concepts.

Unity and Oneness: Here, everything exists in a state of pure energy and consciousness, a singularity where all is connected.

Material: This dimension brings us into the physical world, where we are bound by time and space.

Duality: Our current dwelling place, where light and dark, good and evil, all exist in a dynamic dance.

Spiritual: This dimension links the physical with the spiritual, a fusion of time, space, and consciousness.

Consciousness: A place where the interconnectedness of all life is realized, a profound sense of oneness with everything. Endless possibilities, where the universe's infinite potential resides.

Creativity and Imagination: Here, thoughts and intentions come to life, and we harness the power of creation.

Wisdom: In this realm, we access higher consciousness, unraveling universal truths.

Love: A dimension filled with deep connections to the divine, a place where love binds us all.

Possibilities/Time/Space: Here, every potential reality exists simultaneously, as well as past, present and future a vast ocean of what was, is and what could be.

Parallel Universes: This dimension opens doors to multiple realities and varied existence.

Light Spectrum: A place to connect with the highest levels of divine wisdom, love, quantum field, and more.

Zero point: I like to imagine it as a place where all dualities and polarities meet and merge into pure unity. In this sacred space, all distinctions collapse, and what's left is a state of pure consciousness, balance, and infinite potential. To me this is an intimate experience. It's a place where judgment, separation, and limitations fade away, leaving behind a serene stillness, bliss and joy that resonates with the core of our being. The concept of the zero point may be very multifaceted, much like a gem that reflects light in a multitude of colors. It's a bridge that connects the tangible with the intangible, the formless with the form, the known with the unknown, the finite with the boundless. It's a journey into the heart of the great mystery that envelops all of existence. As we walk our spiritual path, touching this zero point becomes more than a distant goal; it becomes a lived experience. It's a place of inner silence and boundless love, where we find ourselves connected with everything and yet attached to nothing. It's a state of profound inner peace that transcends the hustle and bustle of our everyday lives. Perhaps you've felt a calling towards this zero point. It's a beautiful mystery that invites both contemplation and direct experience. It's not merely a concept to be analyzed but a doorway to deeper wisdom and understanding. In your quiet moments of reflection or during your meditation practice, you might find glimpses of this zero point. Embrace them, for they are invitations to explore deeper realms of consciousness, where true healing and transformation await.

These descriptions are but interpretations and perspectives, a general map of the landscapes we might explore in our spiritual journey and see them differently and that's ok. The essence of these dimensions transcends words, levels, numbers or beings existing within these dimensions. Each person will experience different dimensions, different information, and come into contact with different beings. All is perfect for our own journey and understanding of the universe and what we can bring forth and share with each other from these encounters. The most profound understanding comes from our own inner experiences, connections and navigations amongst these. As we change our vibration, frequency, and consciousness. Let's be open to different ideas and lenses, always seeking, shifting, and striving for a greater connection within ourselves and the world around us.

«We are travelers on a cosmic journey, stardust, swirling and dancing in the eddies and whirlpools of infinity. Life is eternal. We have stopped for a moment to encounter each other, to meet, to love, to share. This is a precious moment. It is a little parenthesis in eternity.» - Paulo Coehlo

CHAPTER 13

THE IDEA THAT TIME IS AN ILLUSION

THE ILLUSION OF LINEAR TIME

L et us embark on a journey that transcends the ordinary understanding of time. Here I share with you an extraordinary perspective where past, present, and future converge, and we, as fractals of the divine, dance through them in harmony.

The Illusion of Linear Time

In our daily lives, we perceive time as a straight line, where the past gives way to the present, and the present leads to the future. But what if this linear perspective is but a limited understanding, an illusion that veils a deeper, more mystical truth?

The Convergence of Time

Imagine for a moment that the past, present, and future are all happening simultaneously, not sequentially. In the grand tapestry of existence, every moment is intertwined, each one alive and vibrant. This notion defies our logical mind but resonates with the wisdom of many spiritual traditions.

Fractals of the Divine

We are more than mere physical beings; we are fractals of the divine, echoes of something far greater. Our essence vibrates with frequency, density, and energy, and these vibrations allow us to exist simultaneously across all timelines. We're not confined to the here and now; we are part of an eternal dance that spans all of existence.

Dancing Through Timelines

As we evolve spiritually, our vibration changes, and this change unlocks doors to new realms of experience. We can find ourselves connected to past wisdom and future possibilities, all while grounded in the present moment. This dance across timelines is not a mere metaphor; it can be a lived experience through practices like meditation, contemplation, and mindful living.

The Gift of Simultaneous Existence

To exist simultaneously across all timelines is to embrace our multidimensional nature. It's to recognize that we are not confined to a single moment but are participants in a cosmic play that transcends ordinary understanding. It's a realization that frees us from the limitations of linear time and invites us to experience a more profound connection with our true selves and the divine.

Embracing the Dance

I invite you to ponder this perspective, to let it stir within your soul. Consider the possibility that time's dance is not a rigid march but a fluid waltz, where past, present, and future embrace in eternal harmony. Perhaps, in your moments of quiet reflection or during your meditation, you might glimpse this timeless dance. If so, embrace it. Allow it to guide you to new depths of understanding and connection. For in this dance, we find not only wisdom but a love that transcends all boundaries, a love that is the very fabric of existence itself.

CHAPTER 14

THE IDEA THAT REALITY IS AN ILLUSION

WE ARE NOT MERE SPECTATORS, BUT ACTIVE PARTICIPANTS.

A sacred dance that involves geometry, patterns, frequency, vibration, magnetism, minerals, synchronicities, and the very essence of the universe. We are not mere spectators but active participants in this cosmic dance, and it's through our senses that we navigate and perceive this physical reality.

Sacred Geometry: The Blueprint of Creation

Sacred geometry, the divine patterns and shapes that permeate existence, is the architect's plan of the cosmos. It's the golden spiral in a seashell, the fractal beauty of a snowflake, the harmonious symmetry of a flower. These patterns are not mere coincidence but a profound language, a way the universe communicates and connects with itself, and with us.

Frequency and Vibration: The Music of the Spheres

All that exists hums with frequency and vibration. It's the resonance of atoms, the pulsing of stars, the rhythm of our hearts. We are all part of this universal orchestra, playing our unique notes. Understanding and aligning with these vibrations allows us to harmonize with the universe, to become co-creators in this magnificent symphony.

Magnetism: The Invisible Embrace

Magnetism, the unseen force that binds and attracts, is a metaphor for the deeper connections that weave us into the fabric of existence. It reminds us that we are never truly separate but interlinked, drawn to each other through unseen but powerful forces, reflecting our spiritual connection.

Minerals: Part of Earth's Wisdom Keepers

The minerals and crystals of our Earth are not just inert matter but wisdom keepers, resonating with ancient knowledge. They hold frequencies, capture light, and reflect beauty in ways that remind us of our own complexity and potential. As part of the Earth, they are part of us too, and they invite us to rediscover our roots and essence.

The Universe Within: A Microcosm of the Macrocosm

We are not just in the universe; the universe is within us. Every star that twinkles, every wave that crashes, every mountain that stands tall – they are echoes of our own being. How we navigate and perceive this reality through our senses is a sacred exploration, a journey inward to the core of existence.

Dancing with the Divine

The path we tread is one of wonder and discovery. The idea that reality is an illusion is not a dismissal of life but an invitation to see it with new eyes. To recognize the sacred geometry, the patterns, the dance of frequency and vibration, the magnetism, the synchronicities, the wisdom of minerals, and the universe within us.

This is a perspective that holds a key to unlock the door of deeper understanding. As you ponder these insights, may you see the world anew, as a magical, interconnected tapestry that sings a song of oneness.

May you dance with the divine, in harmony and joy, ever guided by the love that connects us all. There's an enchanting phenomenon that calls for our attention that is synchronicities. These meaningful synchronicities are whispers from the cosmos, signs that we are intricately linked with the universe in ways that go beyond the surface of physical reality.

Mirrored Patterns: As Above, So Below

The ancient wisdom, «As above, so below; as within, so without,» speaks to the synchronicities between the macrocosm and the microcosm. The spiral galaxies in the night sky mirror the spirals in our DNA. The orbits of the planets echo the electrons dancing around the nucleus. This sacred geometry is a reminder that we are a reflection of the universe, and it is reflected within us.

Resonance and Alignment: The Harmony of Being

Have you ever thought of someone, only to have them contact you that day? Or stumbled upon a quote that speaks to a question you've been pondering? Number sequence, angel number meanings, feathers, and more? These are synchronicities at work, nudges from the universe, guiding us towards alignment and resonance. They're signs that we're in tune with the natural flow of life.

Intuitive Wisdom: The Dance of Knowing

Sometimes, we know something without knowing how we know it. It's a sudden insight, a flash of understanding that seems to come from nowhere and yet feels profoundly right. These intuitive glimpses are synchronicities between our inner wisdom and the wisdom of the universe, a dance of knowing that transcends the mind.

Healing and Transformation: The Alchemy of Growth

Synchronicities often appear at crucial moments in our lives, leading us to healing, transformation, and growth. Whether it's a chance meeting, a dream, or an unexpected opportunity, these cosmic winks are guiding hands, helping us navigate our path with grace and trust.

The Unity of All Things: A Symphony of Connection

Ultimately, synchronicities are a testimony to the underlying unity of all things. They're evidence that the universe and physical reality are not separate realms but a continuous symphony, a dance of connection that we're all part of. It's a living, breathing relationship that invites us to awaken to the magic and mystery of existence.

Embracing the Cosmic Dance

The synchronicities between the universe and physical reality are invitations, gentle taps on the shoulder from the divine, asking us to pay attention, to see the deeper connections, to embrace the cosmic dance. May we walk this path with a heart open to wonder, eyes attuned to the sacred, and a soul resonant with the love that weaves all into one.

CHAPTER 15

THINNING OF THE VEIL OF FORGETFULNESS

A GENTLE AWAKENING

I n our soul's voyage across the infinite expanses of consciousness, we often find ourselves adrift in the human experience, caught between the realms of the divine and the mundane. It is here, within this beautiful dichotomy, that a profound and mysterious process unfolds: the thinning of the veil of forgetfulness, and the ensuing awakening and ascension into our true divine nature and multidimensionality.

The Veil of Forgetfulness: A Sacred Amnesia

When we enter this physical plane, we are wrapped in a veil of forgetfulness, a necessary and divine amnesia that allows us to fully immerse ourselves in the human experience. This veil obscures our true essence, hiding from us the luminous beings of love and light that we are at our core. But why, you might wonder, would we ever choose to forget our divine nature?

The Human Journey: A Divine Experiment

The human journey is a rich tapestry, woven with threads of joy and sorrow, triumph and despair. It's a divine experiment, allowing us to learn, grow, and evolve. By temporarily forgetting our divine origins, we dive deeply into the experience of duality, learning lessons that only this unique existence can offer.

The Thinning Veil: A Gentle Awakening

As we walk our spiritual path, we may begin to sense a softening, a thinning of the veil that separates us from our higher selves. It's a subtle shift, a gentle awakening that calls us back to our divine essence. The lessons of life have prepared us for this moment, and as the veil becomes more transparent, we start to remember our true nature.

Multidimensionality: The Dance of Many Worlds

With the thinning of the veil, we awaken to our multidimensionality. We are not merely human beings having a spiritual experience; we are spiritual beings having a human experience. We begin to perceive the many dimensions and realms that are intertwined with our reality, recognizing that we exist simultaneously across different levels of consciousness.

Ascension: The Return to Divinity

The process of ascension is the natural culmination of this awakening. As we transcend the limitations of our physical selves and the veil continues to dissolve, we embrace our divinity, the pure, radiant love that is our true nature. We return to a state of oneness, a harmonious dance with the cosmos.

REMEMBERING: **A Homecoming of the Soul**

This sacred journey of awakening and ascension is a homecoming. It's a remembering of who we truly are, an unfolding of our innate wisdom and beauty. It's a path filled with wonder, awe, and a profound sense of coming home.

Embracing Your Divine Journey

May you walk this path with grace, courage, and an open heart. Know that you are guided, supported, and loved beyond measure. The thinning of the veil of forgetfulness is an invitation to awaken to your true self, to remember your divinity and the dazzling multidimensionality of your being. The thinning of the veil of forgetfulness is not something to fear but a call to remember, a sacred invitation to return to our true selves.

The Dance of Life: Pushing, Pulling, Resistance, and the Grace of Flow State and Acceptance

In our magnificent journey through life, we often find ourselves caught between the forces of pushing and pulling, resistance and flow. I went through this and could not understand when to do what. The reason for this, I found out later, is because I was not in tune with my higher self. I was not grounded and in tune with my soul and my guides. I was only focusing on the external world and trying to control it. This quickly became very depleting in every aspect and difficult to maintain in the long run. These energies, both tangible and intangible, shape our experiences and guide our paths in ways both subtle and profound. Let's explore this dance and learn to recognize when we're forcing life and when we're flowing with it, for within this understanding lies profound wisdom and peace.

. . .

«Where focus goes, energy flows. And where energy flows, whatever you're focusing on grows. In other words, your life is controlled by what you focus on. That's why you need to focus on where you want to go, not on what you fear.» -Tony Robbins

Pushing: The Desire to Control

We all have moments where we try to push life in the direction we want it to go. We strive, we grasp, we exert effort, driven by our desires and fears. Pushing can sometimes feel like the right thing to do. After all, we are often taught that effort and control are the pathways to success. But is this always the case?

Pulling: The Yearning for More

Pulling is another aspect of this intricate dance. We might find ourselves constantly yearning, longing for something more, something different. This pulling can manifest as dissatisfaction or a sense of lack, and it keeps us reaching for something just out of our grasp.

Resistance: The Wall of Fear

Resistance is like a wall we build out of our fears, doubts, and insecurities. It's a protective barrier, but it can also become a prison. Resistance keeps us stuck, unable to move forward or back, trapped in a pattern that doesn't serve our higher selves.

Flow State: The Grace of Letting Go

In contrast to pushing, pulling, and resistance, there's the flow state, a state of grace, ease, and alignment with the natural rhythm of life. When we are in flow, we are not forcing or struggling; we are simply being, allowing life to unfold as it will, trusting that we are where we need to be.

You become the observer, as consciousness you can observe the passing thoughts, emotions, and circumstances knowing they are transient. It is just an opportunity to help you remember your true self, your essence.

The Dance: Finding Your Rhythm

Life is a delicate dance between these forces. There's a time for pushing, a time for pulling, a time for resisting, and a time for flowing. The wisdom lies in recognizing which energy is needed when. Sometimes, we must push through barriers to grow. Sometimes, we must pull ourselves up and strive for more. Sometimes, resistance shows us where we need to heal. And sometimes, flow is the path to true fulfillment.

Embracing the Journey: From Struggle to Harmony

As we become more attuned to these energies, we learn to move from struggle to harmony. We learn when to push and when to let go, when to pull and when to surrender. We discover the profound peace that comes from aligning with the natural rhythms of life.

The Wisdom of the Dance

May you find the grace to flow, the courage to push, the inspiration to pull, and the wisdom to recognize when resistance is guiding you to deeper understanding. Embrace the dance of life, for it is within this beautiful interplay of forces that we find our true selves, our purpose, and our joy.

I hope these words serve as a gentle reminder that life's struggles and ease are both part of our spiritual journey.

Understanding the dynamics of pushing, pulling, resistance, and flow can lead us to a more conscious and harmonious way of living. May you dance with life, not against it, and find the grace that lies in each step.

Bending Space and Time - A Journey Through the Fabric of Reality

Let us embark on an exploration into a concept that marries both science and spirituality, the bending of space and time. This captivating idea offers us a glimpse into the profound connection between the physical universe and the realm of consciousness.

Gravity: The Dance of the Cosmos

In the breathtaking theory of relativity, we discover that gravity is not merely a force between two objects. It's something far more poetic. Massive objects like stars and planets curve the fabric of space and time, creating a gravitational embrace that guides the dance of everything within their influence. It's a cosmic ballet, where space and time yield to the presence of mass and energy.

Time Dilation: The Relativity of Time

Have you ever felt time slipping through your fingers or stretching out before you? In the world of relativity, time itself is flexible. Depending on the pull of gravity or the speed of movement, time can stretch or contract. This phenomenon, known as time dilation, has implications not just for the world of physics but also for our understanding of the transient nature of existence.

Wormholes: Portals Through Spacetime

The curvature of spacetime invites us to dream about the possibility of wormholes, those magical bridges between realms. Though still in the realm of speculation, the idea of wormholes tantalizes the imagination with possibilities of travel beyond the limitations of our known universe. How thrilling to ponder that we might one day traverse the vast cosmos in an instant and what if meditation was one way to do this!

Black Holes: Vortices of Mystery

Black holes are regions of spacetime where gravity pulls so much that even light cannot escape. They are the ultimate cosmic traps, absorbing everything that comes too close. The interior of a black hole, hidden behind an event horizon, remains one of the most puzzling mysteries in science.

Black holes may be seen as symbols of transformation and renewal. While they devour everything within reach, they also play a vital role in shaping galaxies. Could they be cosmic crucibles where the old is consumed, allowing the new to be born? We find a beautiful interplay between the physical and metaphysical. These cosmic phenomena challenge our understanding of the universe and invite us to explore our spiritual connection to all that is.

Beyond the Physical Plane

Now, let's transcend the boundaries of science and embrace the spiritual facet of bending space and time. This concept, as complex as it is, resonates with many spiritual teachings that speak of the power of consciousness to transcend the physical. Could it be that bending space and time is not just a scientific marvel but also a metaphor for our ability to ascend to higher realms of awareness, consciousness, and other dimensions?

From the perspective I have at this moment, to ascend in

consciousness is simply recognizing oneself and one's true essence. So essentially you already are that which you are looking for, you have simply purposely forgotten momentarily to enjoy and be fully immersed in this spirit-human journey. You are the universe/Source/ God/creation experiencing itself from infinite points, fractals, forms, which allows you to become aware of life and creation from different perspectives in the case of human from the material, experiential, ever expanding senses form.

Could we, as spiritual beings, learn to navigate the folds of our reality?

In the dance of infinite possibilities, we find echoes of our search for meaning, connection, and transcendence. They serve as reminders that our multi-verse is not just a physical entity but a spiritual landscape filled with lessons, symbols, and inspiration. May you continue to explore these cosmic marvels with a heart full of curiosity and a soul touched and guided by the divine.

A Unified Perspective: The Harmony of Science and Spirituality

In this exploration, we find that bending space and time is not confined to the domain of science. It reaches into the depths of our soul, beckoning us to reflect on our place in the cosmos, our connection to the divine, and our potential to transcend the ordinary. It's a beautiful fusion of science and spirituality that enriches our understanding of ourselves and the universe.

«The day science begins to study non-physical phenomena, it will make more progress in one decade than in all the previous centuries of its existence.» — Nikola Tesla

I INVITE you to carry the wonder of bending space and time into your daily contemplation, especially through meditation. Let it inspire you to question, explore, and marvel at the intricacy of existence. For in the dance of the cosmos, the flexibility of time, the allure of wormholes, blackholes and the spiritual resonance of these concepts, we find reflections of our multifaceted reality. May the mysteries of space and time continue to enchant and guide you on your spiritual journey. Embracing both the scientific marvel and spiritual essence of bending space and time, we open ourselves to a world full of wonder, connection, and infinite possibilities. It's a testament to the profound relationship between our tangible reality and the intangible realm of consciousness.

CHAPTER 16

TIME TRAVEL AND OUT OF BODY EXPERIENCES

THE EXPERIENCE OF OUR CONSCIOUSNESS JOURNEYING BEYOND OUR PHYSICAL FORM

W e'll explore some fascinating concepts that stretch the boundaries of our understanding, including time travel, out of body experiences, astral travel, and shamanic journeying.

«There is a world beyond ours, a world that is far away, nearby and invisible» - María Sabina

Time Travel: A Journey Beyond Linearity

Time travel has captivated human imagination for centuries. From the standpoint of physics, it's a theoretical possibility, entangled with the mysteries of gravity and the relative nature of time. Einstein's theory of relativity opened our eyes to the idea that time is not an absolute entity but is linked to space, forming a four-dimensional fabric known as spacetime.

From a spiritual angle, the notion that time is an illusion is embraced by many traditions. Time as we perceive it may not be linear; instead, all moments could exist simultaneously. By transcending our ordinary perceptions through practices like meditation, we might glimpse a reality that transcends our normal experience of linear time.

Astral Travel: Exploring the Boundless Self Astral travel

The experience of our consciousness journeying beyond our physical form, has long been a topic in various spiritual traditions. Whether seeking guidance, exploring past lives, or simply yearning to understand the universe more deeply, this form of non-physical travel offers a unique pathway.

These experiences, often cultivated through deep relaxation, visualization, or trance, allow us to navigate dimensions not normally accessible. The validity and nature of astral travel remain debated topics, but they continue to provide rich insights into the human psyche and our relationship with the cosmos.

Shamanic Journeying: Connecting with the Spiritual Realms

Shamanic journeying brings us into the world of indigenous wisdom, where altered states of consciousness provide gateways to spiritual knowledge. Using techniques like drumming and chanting, shamans and practitioners travel to non-ordinary states of consciousness.

These journeys offer opportunities for self-discovery, healing, and profound connections with spiritual guides or teachers. Far from being confined to ancient traditions, shamanic journeying resonates with many today, offering a tangible connection to the wisdom of our ancestors and the heartbeat of the Earth.

A Harmonious Symphony

What binds these diverse concepts together is the human quest to transcend limitations, explore the unknown, and deepen our connection with the spiritual realms. Our yearning to bend the fabric of spacetime, journey beyond our physical selves, or access ancient wisdom through shamanic practices reflects our innate desire to understand the nature of reality.

These ideas challenge our conventional perspectives, offering us glimpses of a reality that are far more complex and interconnected than we might ordinarily perceive. They invite us to stretch our minds, open our hearts, and embark on journeys of discovery that may transform not only our understanding of the universe, but also our place within it.

Whether approached through science, spirituality, or a blend of both, these concepts continue to fascinate and inspire. They beckon us to set aside preconceived notions, to explore with curiosity and wonder, and to embrace the mysteries of existence. May our journeys through time and space bring us closer to the ultimate truths of who we are and the infinite potentials that lie within us all.

Out-of-body experiences (OBEs) are profound and mysterious phenomena where an individual perceives themselves as separate from their physical body. These occurrences can happen spontaneously, during sleep, or be induced through various techniques or practices.

Unlike dreams or fantasies, those who have experienced OBEs often describe them as incredibly vivid and real. Some interpret these experiences as a journey of the soul or consciousness, moving beyond the confines of the physical body.

From a scientific perspective, OBEs are complex phenomena often associated with altered states of consciousness. Some researchers link them to specific brain activities, while others explore them within the context of mystical and transcendental experiences.

In many spiritual traditions, OBEs are considered a form of astral travel, allowing one to explore different realms and dimensions. They might offer insights into our true nature, helping us understand that we are more than just our physical selves.

Integrating Out-of-Body Experiences (OBEs), along with the concepts of time travel, astral travel, and shamanic journeying, paint a picture of a reality far more intricate and multidimensional than our day-to-day experience. They are reminders that our physical senses only perceive a fragment of the grand symphony that is existence.

Whether we view OBEs through the lens of spirituality, science, or both, they provide us with a unique opportunity to explore the very nature of consciousness and reality. They invite us to transcend our physical limitations and engage with the universe in a more profound and interconnected way.

These experiences might also be seen as a metaphor for our spiritual journey. As we navigate the paths of self-discovery, healing, and growth, we are continually moving beyond the known, stretching our awareness, and connecting with dimensions of ourselves and the universe previously unexplored.

In our exploration of time travel, astral travel, shamanic journeying, and out-of-body experiences, we are confronted with the vastness of what it means to be human. We are beings capable of transcending time, space, and physicality, journeying into realms that provide wisdom, connection, and enlightenment. May these concepts inspire you to seek, question, and journey with an open heart and curious mind. In doing so, you may find doors within yourself leading to landscapes of beauty, understanding, and infinite possibilities. In the words of Rumi:

«You are not a drop in the ocean. You are the entire ocean, in a drop.»

In our shared journey through life's mysteries, we often seek connections and wisdom that bind us to the universe. One of the deepest sources of this wisdom springs from the indigenous knowledge cultivated over millennia. Allow me to guide you through the indigenous view of the universe, where everything is part of a living, interconnected system.

CHAPTER 17

INDIGENOUS PEOPLE AS EARTH AND WISDOM KEEPERS

THE UNIVERSE AS A LIVING SYSTEM

There's a profound understanding among indigenous peoples that they are the keepers of Earth's wisdom. They act as stewards of the land, preserving ancient knowledge and practices that respect and nourish the Earth and the universe. This role as wisdom keepers is not merely a responsibility; it is a sacred trust, a spiritual calling to protect and honor the planet that sustains us all. I feel we have so much to learn from each other, from every religion, from every culture, from every practice, if we would focus more on our similarities and contribution to a more sustainable co-existence, this would allow us to live in peace from our heart and our true expression.

«The touch of an infinite mystery passes over the trivial and the familiar, making it break out into an ineffable music...The trees, the stars, and the blue hills ache with a meaning which can never be uttered in words.» - Rabindranath Tagore.

THE UNIVERSE as a Living System

The indigenous perspective sees every element such as rocks, rivers, animals and humans as part of a grand web of life. This view informs every aspect of their lives, helping them recognize the circle of life that connects us all. Through dances, prayers, and offerings, indigenous people connect with the universe and honor the spirits of the natural world. These rituals are paths to understanding the universe, not just traditional customs. The stories that pass through generations weave the rich fabric of indigenous cultures. They are timeless reminders of our interconnectedness and the wisdom inherent in nature.

The Relationship between Indigenous People and the Land

The land is sacred to indigenous people. Their spiritual connection with the Earth is not just a belief but a way of life that inspires respect, reverence and stewardship. Despite the trials brought by colonialism, globalization and climate change, the resilience of indigenous people shines through. Their role as Earth's wisdom keepers continues to inspire them to champion social and environmental justice. Indigenous wisdom is not in conflict with modern science but can complement and enhance our approach to global challenges.

The insights from these wisdom keepers guide us toward sustainable and harmonious living.

The Importance of Cultural Diversity

We must treasure the rich diversity of indigenous cultures, respecting and celebrating the unique knowledge they offer. They are a wellspring of different ways of relating to the world and one another. By engaging in open dialogue and learning from the wisdom keepers of the Earth, we can create a harmonious, equitable and sustainable future. Their insights offer a guide to living in accord with nature and each other.

Indigenous people stand as guardians of the Earth and keepers of timeless wisdom. Their understanding of the universe invites us to live with greater harmony, respect, and awareness. Let us heed their teachings, for they offer a path to a deeper connection with the natural world and guide us toward a more just and sustainable future for all. May this inspire you to explore the wisdom and lessons that indigenous earth and wisdom keepers offer. Their insights are not only a testament to the richness of their cultures but also a beacon to all of humanity, illuminating a way of life that reveres the Earth and recognizes the sacredness of all existence.

«**What if our religion were each other?**

If our practice was our life?

If prayer was our words?

What if the Temple was the Earth?

If the forests were our church?

If holy water were the rivers, lakes and oceans?

What if meditation was our relationships?

If the teacher was life?

If the wisdom was self-knowledge?

If love was the center of our being?»

-Ganga White

Healing with the Plants of the Amazon: Sacred Plant Medicine

Through the heart of the Amazon and the soul of ancient traditions. We can explore the sacred realms of plant medicine and embark on a profound adventure that connects us to the roots of human wisdom, healing, and spiritual connection. This is for informational purposes only. I am not recommending you do any psychedelics or non-psychedelic work with plants and the opinion on this book does not replace professional advice and treatment from your healthcare providers.

In the mystical embrace of the Amazon rainforest, we discover a treasure trove of plant species that the indigenous communities have revered for centuries as sacred medicine. These beautiful plants, bearing the wisdom of nature, spirit, and much more offer profound healing for both our physical and spiritual ailments.

Each is unique, sacred, and with so much love and so

many teachings and lessons that can help us in our unique journey. Each plant has its own essence, soul, spirit, unique energy and vibration to it. It's like having access to many different teachers each with their own unique style of teaching all from love and with love and the utmost respect on both sides. Each plant offers unique pathways to spiritual understanding and healing. They are sacred tools for self-discovery, providing wisdom and insights. Their use is not to be taken lightly. Proper guidance, respect for tradition, and careful preparation are crucial for those seeking to explore these spiritual medicines.

Ayahuasca: The Vine of the Soul

Ayahuasca, the renowned brew of the Amazon, is a spiritual elixir that connects the mind and heart. Through the weaving of the ayahuasca vine and chacruna leaves, a doorway is opened to profound healing, self-discovery, and spiritual insight. In various indigenous cultures, Ayahuasca is considered a sacrament, bridging the physical and spiritual worlds. Shamans and healers use it to gain insights, cleanse the soul, and communicate with other realms. It often induces intense, visionary experiences that are deeply transformative. Modern studies are exploring Ayahuasca's potential in treating mental health issues like depression, anxiety, PTSD and much more. Its profound impact on emotional healing and self-awareness is attracting interest from medical communities worldwide.

The Sacred Cactus: San Pedro

San Pedro, known as huachuma, stands tall in the Andean regions, serving as a symbol of growth. Its psychedelic compound, mescaline, induces profound spiritual experiences. Used by the Andean shamans, San Pedro is often referred to as the «grandfather medicine». It's believed to connect individuals to the earth and cosmos, teaching wisdom, empathy, and compassion. It's a gentle guide to self-realization and spiritual awakening. Traditionally used for healing both physical and emotional ailments, San Pedro might help alleviate anxiety and depression, fostering a sense of inner peace.

Tobacco: The Sacred Breath

Tobacco is more than a plant; it's a spiritual companion. Its deep connection to shamanic rituals and medicinal practices reveals a world of healing and spiritual engagement.

Mapacho, a type of tobacco (*Nicotiana rustica*), is deeply intertwined with South American indigenous practices. For many shamans, Mapacho is a spiritual ally, facilitating communication with the spirit world and used to cleanse energies. The smoke of Mapacho is believed to carry prayers to the divine, opening pathways to wisdom and clarity. Mapacho's stimulating effects may enhance focus and cognitive function. It has been used for various ailments, including respiratory and digestive issues, embodying both the strength and gentleness of Mother Nature.

Lupuna: The Sacred Tree of Wisdom

Lupuna, a majestic tree of the Amazon, is a sacred symbol in indigenous beliefs. Its healing virtues, spiritual significance, and potential therapeutic benefits are woven into the fabric of traditional practices. Lupuna, or Ceiba pentandra, is a towering tree in the Amazon, often referred to as the «Mother of the Forest.» In many indigenous traditions, Lupuna is a symbol of strength and grounding. It's believed to be a wise and protective spirit, guiding those who seek to understand life's mysteries. The energy of Lupuna is considered nurturing and is often invoked for spiritual protection. While not as commonly used in physical healing, the presence and energy of Lupuna in spiritual ceremonies may bring mental clarity and emotional stability, assisting in personal growth.

Kambo: The Amazonian giant leaf frog

Kambo secretes a substance that's rich in peptides, known for its healing properties. Indigenous tribes in the Amazon have used Kambo for generations. Kambo is believed to cleanse the spirit and body of negative energies. In traditional shamanic rituals, it's applied through burns on the skin, facilitating a deep purging process. This purification is said to align the physical and spiritual self, strengthening the connection to nature and the universe. Beyond spiritual healing, Kambo is known to boost the immune system, alleviate depression, anxiety, and pain. Its potent peptides are considered a natural way to detoxify the body and mind, promoting overall well-being.

Ajo Sacha

Ajo Sacha, it's often used in protective rituals, warding off negative energies. The plant's essence is said to align one with their true path and facilitate spiritual growth. Ajo Sacha has been employed to treat respiratory problems and skin conditions. Its anti-inflammatory properties make it a potent natural remedy for various ailments.

Acacia

Acacia, particularly its bark, is rich in DMT, a compound associated with profound spiritual experiences. Acacia's spiritual properties lie in its ability to open doors to other realms. Many regard it as a key to unlocking deep spiritual insights and awakening higher consciousness. It's being explored for potential mental health benefits, possibly aiding in the healing of depression and anxiety through guided spiritual journeys.

Blue Lotus

The blue lotus holds a sacred place in ancient Egyptian culture. Associated with divinity and enlightenment, blue lotus has been depicted in many ancient artifacts as a symbol of purity and spiritual growth. Its ethereal blue petals are seen as a gateway to higher understanding. It has been used as a mild sedative and may promote a sense of tranquility and peace, aiding meditation and inner clarity.

Yerba Santa

Yerba Santa is a sacred plant in Native American traditions. Known as the «Holy Herb», Yerba Santa is used to purify spaces and individuals. It can clear away lingering negative energies, creating a sacred space for spiritual connection. Medicinally, Yerba Santa has been employed for respiratory issues, fever, and digestive problems. Its healing nature extends beyond the physical, touching the very soul of those who seek its wisdom.

These sacred plants to name a few and many more provide a profound connection to nature's wisdom and spiritual insight. Their use is not merely for physical healing but to guide the seeker towards higher truths and deeper understanding. Respecting their sacred nature and the traditions from which they originate is essential in approaching them. They remind us of the intricate connection between the body, mind and spirit, offering wisdom that transcends our ordinary perception. As we walk the path of spiritual exploration, may we honor and learn from these sacred teachers of the earth, embracing their lessons with gratitude and reverence.

Embracing the "«God Molecule»: DMT

In our exploration, we'll also touch on dimethyltryptamine (DMT), often referred to as the «God molecule.» This compound, transcending ordinary consciousness, offers mystical experiences that connect us to the divine within and without.

DMT is a naturally occurring psychedelic substance found in various plants and animals, including the previously mentioned Acacia.

Spiritual Significance

Often referred to as the «Spirit Molecule,» DMT induces intense, otherworldly experiences. Many who have ventured into a DMT journey report encounters with entities, profound insights, and a sensation of unity with the universe. It's a substance that transcends the physical world, providing glimpses into unseen realms. Research on DMT's therapeutic benefits is still in its infancy, but some studies suggest it may help in treating addiction and mental health disorders. Its powerful effect on consciousness can lead to transformative healing experiences.

The journey into sacred plant medicine is not without complexities, risks and responsibilities. You must consider the right facilitator, the right setting, right dose, the right support, integration process and I invite you to do your own research if this is something that is aligned with you. This is for information purposes only. I am not suggesting you work with these medicines as this is an individual journey for each one of us that creates our collective ever changing and expanding reality. These plant teachers and sacred substances continue to intrigue and inspire those who walk the path of spiritual exploration. They are reminders of the profound connection we share with the earth and all living beings, a connection that calls us to wisdom, compassion, and the never-ending journey of self-discovery. Sacred plant medicine offers us a mirror to our soul, a healer for our wounds, and a guide to our spiritual path. In embracing the wisdom of the Amazon and the teachings of indigenous traditions, we honor the interconnectedness of all life. May this journey inspire us to walk with reverence, compassion, and humility. Let us also remember to preserve the sanctity of these traditions, the well-being of the Amazon rainforest, and the rights of the indigenous communities.

«Earth Mother, you who are called by a thousand names. May all remember we are cells in your body and dance together.» - Starhawk.

CHAPTER 18

BIODIVERSITY

THE HEARTBEAT OF EARTH

B iodiversity is the soulful dance of life. It reflects the diversity of species, ecosystems and genetic uniqueness within each being. Like notes in a divine melody, each organism plays its role in the orchestration of existence. Each species is a link in the great chain of being. The disappearance of even one can cause ripples that disturb the entire cosmic dance and ecosystem. Think of bees, those humble pollinators whose loss would echo through our fields and orchards. Reflect on wolves, whose absence would disrupt the balance of their realms. The trees, waters, and winds whisper blessings to us in the form of air purification, climate regulation, and soil fertility. These gifts flow to us from the bosom of Mother Nature, and they sustain us physically and spiritually.

Many of our brothers and sisters around the world find solace, wisdom, and communion with the divine in the arms of nature. Our souls are nurtured by the beauty, complexity, and sacred geometry of life's manifold expressions. We stand as stewards of this magical symphony. Biodiversity is not merely a biological concept; it is a spiritual testament to our moral and ethical responsibility to safeguard the divine dance of life. From the forest's heart, we derive medicines and cures that heal our bodies. In diversity lies strength. Rich ecosystems endure storms and calamities with grace. We are nurtured by the fruits of biodiversity, and in return, we must nurture it and protect the earth for ourselves and for the generations to come.

We must walk with reverence, recognizing that our actions today weave the fabric of tomorrow's world. Biodiversity is the essence of our existence, a cosmic symphony where each note resonates with purpose and meaning. From the humblest insect to the mightiest tree, from the sacred plants that guide our spiritual journeys to the unseen microbes that sustain our soils - all are part of this wondrous dance. May we embrace our roles as conscious co-creators, nurturing and protecting the richness of life, and honoring the sacred wisdom that whispers in the wind, flows in the rivers, and blooms in every heart.

Looking at life as Birth and Rebirth cycles

In our walk through the path of existence as souls and time travelers we encounter a profound and beautiful perspective: Life is a series of cycles, an endless dance of birth, growth, transformation, and renewal. Each step we take is a part of this magnificent journey and each cycle we move through is an invitation to deepen our connection with ourselves, each other, and the cosmos.

THE DANCE of Birth and Rebirth

From the moment we take our first breath to the time we transition into new realms, we are engaged in a continual process of birth and rebirth. Just as a flower blossoms, withers, and blooms again, so do we go through cycles of unfolding and returning. Each cycle in our lives, be it a new relationship, career, or personal awakening, offers lessons and challenges. These are not mere events that seem to have happened without any deliberate plan or caused by mere chance. Although some may appear to be random or accidental, they may have a deeper significance, carrying a sense of unexpected alignment and synchronicity in life's events. These are divine invitations to expand our awareness and enrich our spiritual understanding of events.

Within the many traditions that grace our world, the concept of rebirth is often linked to the soul's journey through various stages of consciousness. This journey, filled with learning and discovery, leads us toward growth, ascension, expansion and union with the divine. Look around and you will see the dance of birth and rebirth mirrored in nature. The seasons change, the moon and the Earth breathes in rhythms that are both ancient and eternal. By aligning with these natural cycles, we harmonize with the universe.

Change can be both a source of excitement and a cause for trepidation. But in recognizing the cyclical nature of life, we come to see change not as something to fear but as a natural and necessary part of our human experience. As we approach each new cycle, let us do so with open hearts and curious minds. Each phase is a new chapter, a new adventure filled with potential and possibility. By honoring the cycles within us and around us, we find balance. Just as the tides ebb and flow, so do our emotions, thoughts, and energies. Embrace this dance, for it is the rhythm of life itself. The cycles of birth and rebirth teach us to move with grace and understanding. They remind us that every ending is a new beginning, that every challenge is an opportunity for growth, and that every moment is a chance to love more deeply.

The dance of birth and rebirth is a sacred and profound aspect of our spiritual journey. It is a constant reminder that we are part of something vast and eternal, connected to the cycles of nature and the pulse of the universe. As we embrace this perspective, we unlock doors of wisdom and compassion. We learn to see life not as a linear path but as a spiral, ever moving, ever growing, ever returning to the Source of all creation. May we all dance this dance with joy, courage, and love, trusting that each step, each cycle, is a blessing and a gift.

Have you ever sat under a canopy of stars and wondered about the fabric of the universe? At the heart of it all, every twinkle of starlight, every gust of wind, and even the very essence of «you» is pulsating with energy.

CHAPTER 19

A DIFFERENT WAY OF HEALING

HEAL YOURSELF

Quantum Healing

Quantum Healing is a concept that might sound straight out of a sci-fi novel, but it's deeply spiritual. The idea is simple, yet profound. Picture this: Everything in our vast universe, down to the very core of our being is made up of energy. Our universe, with its vast galaxies and us, beings within it and it being within us, we operate on principles of energy. Imagine for a moment that your body isn't just flesh, bones, and blood. Instead, it's a symphony of energies, singing and dancing in harmony.

In the realm of quantum healing, we believe that sometimes this harmonious tune might face a little discord. Maybe an energy string plucked wrong or a note missed. And this is where ailments, be it of the mind, body, or spirit, might creep in. But fear not, for just as a musician knows how to tune her instrument, there are ways to recalibrate our energies. Through meditative practices, visual journeys, channeling energy, and other energy work we attempt to reconnect with our inner symphony and restore balance. This is not to be replaced by your usual medical treatment but in collaboration with it.

Now as we tread this path of exploration, it's essential to view quantum healing and other perspectives with curiosity like a child and not with judgment. I encourage you to approach quantum healing or any other form of healing or energy work with an open heart and an inquiring mind. Marry the wisdom of ancient spiritual practices with the marvels of modern science. Listen to your inner voice, but also, don't shy away from seeking advice from the pillars of contemporary medicine. Remember, the universe is vast and mysterious, and every day, we learn a little more about its enchanting song. Embrace the journey, for it's the exploration that truly heals.

Healing with vibration

I'd like you to feel the rhythm, not just hear it. Let's immerse ourselves in the gentle embrace of vibrations and frequencies that our universe offers. Sound carries the profound essence of Source, creation, healing and transformation.

Have you ever felt calm after listening to a soothing piece of music or the rhythmic beat of a drum? Our universe sings through instruments like singing bowls, gongs, tuning forks, drums, our voice, music, and more. These melodies, rich in vibrations, speak to our soul, relaxing our nervous system, melting away tension, releasing and transmuting trauma and bringing in harmony and balance. They communicate with different parts of our body and resonate with our chakras, rejuvenating, healing and aligning us.

The magical world of music is so vast. From a drumbeat to a serene piano piece, it's not just a series of notes but a canvas of emotions, moods, and memories. The therapeutic essence of music can be our sanctuary. It can lift our spirits, drown our sorrows, and be our companion in solitude, guiding our emotional and spiritual journey. The universe's energy dances around us and within us. Music and instruments let us waltz with this energy of love. Through music and energy work the gentle touch or mere intention, practitioners channel and balance this life force, breaking barriers, rejuvenating our spirits, and invoking our body's innate power to heal.

The Primal Beat of Drums:

Drums, the heartbeat of our ancestors, echo a language older than words. They pulse through ceremonies, celebrations, and meditative practices, connecting us to the earth, to the community, and to our deepest selves. When we drum, or when we're engulfed in its rhythm, we're uniting with a timeless tradition that heals, empowers, and ignites our spirit.

Healing with Frequency and Hertz (Hz):

From binaural beats to the whispers of ancient Solfeggio frequencies, to the visionary rhythms of Rife frequencies, each has its unique song and story. As we resonate with these frequencies and dance to the beats of ancient drums, let's ensure we are attuned to the wisdom of both ancient traditions and modern insights. In this dance of life, vibrations, frequencies, and the compelling beats of drums invite us to sway, leap, and twirl. Let's embrace the music with an open heart, guided feet, and a curious soul.

Healing with the sea

I want to share a little secret with you that has been a part of my personal healing journey- the sea. There's just something about the vast, rhythmic, and mysterious ocean that seems to whisper age-old secrets of wellness and restoration.

Bathing in Nature's Liquid Embrace:

Every time I submerge myself in the gentle embrace of the sea, I feel a connection to something ancient and nurturing. The sea water, brimming with nature's minerals like magnesium, potassium, and iodine, dances on my skin, revitalizing my body. If you've ever struggled with skin issues like eczema or psoriasis, the sea might offer you relief. There's a different kind of magic in the sea breeze. Inhaling deeply, the fresh sea air fills my lungs, feels invigorating, and purifies my spirit. Coastal air, infused with those joyous negative ions, seems to uplift my mood and energize my very being. I've seen friends with allergies and/or asthma feel more open and comfortable breathing by the sea. It's like Mother Nature's own respiratory therapy.

Barefoot Walks & Earthly Connections

One of my favorite activities is a soulful walk on the beach, or elsewhere in nature, the feet sinking slightly into the soft sand, grounding my spirit to the Earth. Have you ever felt that? This beautiful sensation of being rooted and connected? It's known as grounding or earthing, and for me, it's a bridge between the physical and the ethereal, bringing about a sense of peace, improved sleep, and well-being.

Beyond the physical, the sea and nature invites us to a deeper, more spiritual connection. Close your eyes, listen to the waves, feel the salty breeze, and embrace the vast horizon. It's a meditative experience, an intimate dialogue between your soul and the universe, encouraging relaxation and an indescribable bond with nature. While the sea's embrace is therapeutic and soul-enriching, always keep it mindful and remember, it's a complement to our healing journey.

«The cure for anything is salt water: sweat, tears or the sea.» (Isak Dinesen)

Healing with nature

The transformative magic of nature. It's not just about the green trees or the gentle breeze; it's about immersing ourselves in Mother Earth's embrace to experience profound healing and rejuvenation. Have you ever lost yourself in the profound stillness of a forest? Simply being in the woods, soaking in the serene ambiance. Every breath in these green sanctuaries reduces stress, lifts our spirits, and even helps stabilize our blood pressure. It's a soulful dance between us, the trees, mother earth and everything around us.

Nature walks are my go-to. Not just for the physical movement, but for the nourishment they offer my soul. As we wander on these trails, the fresh air fills our lungs, and the sunlight kisses our skin, reviving our physical body. And beyond the physical, there's an ineffable sense of peace that envelops us, away from the tumult of our daily lives.

Gardening is a connection, a meditation, a therapy.

Nurturing plants and watching them grow offers a unique solace and a poignant lesson in patience and growth. For those seeking a more structured path, horticultural therapy offers beautiful avenues to blend the world of plants with emotional and cognitive healing. Nature, in all her glory, offers the perfect backdrop for mindfulness, meditation, and healing. Picture this: you're seated on soft grass, the wind rustling leaves around, and you're deeply attuned to every sound, scent, and sensation. This mindful connection amplifies our inner peace and provides mental clarity.

Nature is a return to our roots, a reminder of the intricate web of life we are part of.

«Not only do we live amongst the stars, the stars live within us.» - Neil deGrasse Tyson

It humbles, heals, and elevates. So, whether it's a brief moment with a blooming flower or days spent in the wilderness, let's pledge to weave nature into our healing journey. Let the dance with Mother Earth begin!

«Let us first be as simple and well as nature ourselves, dispel the clouds which hang over our brows, and take up a little life into our pores...endeavoring to become one of the worthies of the world.» - Henry David Thoreau

The Elemental Embrace: Dancing with Earth, Air, Fire, and Water

Dipping our toes into the ancient currents that have always pulsed through us. Picture this: the four elements –

Earth, Air, Fire, and Water. They're more than just terms, they're the rhythms to which our hearts beat, the songs of our very essence.

The Earth: in all its nurturing glory, has been our anchor and guardian. Every time I feel the pull of chaos, or the weight of the world becomes just a tad too heavy, I seek refuge in Earth's embrace. This could be the simple act of walking barefoot on dew-kissed grass, planting flowers and feeling the soil slip through my fingers, or just lying on the ground, hugging a tree, soaking up its silent wisdom. Earth, my dear friends, is our reminder to stay rooted, yet still reach for the skies. Pachamama mother earth is not just a deity in the traditional sense but also a symbol of the interconnectedness of all life, the mutual dependence between humans and nature and the respect and gratitude we owe to the planet that sustains us. Everything has some level of consciousness although we may not be able to perceive it. Gaia mother earth has a soul, has consciousness and gracefully allows us to co-exist and expand our awareness of consciousness, soul evolution and the evolution of the species as a whole together with her.

«Consciousness sleeps in minerals. It dreams in plants. It wakes in animals and has the potential to become self-aware in humans.» - Rumi

The Air: there's an invisible dance always happening within us and around us, and that's the ballet of the air. Every inhale brings in renewed energy, hopes, and every exhale is a release of the old. The life force inside of us.

Whenever my thoughts cloud my clarity, I head to where the breeze can play with my hair. I let it carry away my worries. Sometimes, I just sit, focusing on the gentle rhythm of my breathing, I practice different types of breathwork, I immerse myself in the air's wisdom. Air is our cue to make space, to be expansive, and to communicate from the heart.

The Fire: It represents that divine spark, that twinkle in our eyes, that restless spirit that pushes us towards our dreams. Whenever I need to reignite my inner flame, I bask in the golden glow of sunrise or lose myself in the hypnotic dance of a campfire. Fire reminds us to be alive, to be passionate, and to transform with grace. I use the violet flame and golden light for healing, as sacred fires. I work with grandfather fire and open my heart to receiving wisdom.

The water: there's the serene wisdom of water. Much like emotions, it can be still or turbulent. When I'm seeking emotional clarity or a refreshing cleanse for my spirit, I head to the water. Whether it's listening to a bubbling brook, soaking in a calming bath, or letting ocean waves kiss my feet, water is my touchstone for introspection and rejuvenation.

Our lives are beautifully intertwined with these elements, not just in the physical sense but in their ethereal wisdom. When we dance with them, embrace their qualities, and let them guide our daily actions and thoughts, we're aligning ourselves with the ageless rhythms of existence. So, let's join hands and twirl in this elemental dance, finding our balance, our joy, and our place in this grand tapestry of life.

«Heal yourself with the light of the sun and the rays of the moon. With the sound of the river and the waterfall. With the swaying of the sea and the fluttering of birds. Heal yourself with mint, neem, and eucalyptus. Sweetened with lavender, rosemary, and chamomile. Hug yourself with cocoa bean and a hint of cinnamon. Put love and tea instead of sugar and drink it looking at the stars. Heal yourself with the kisses the wind gives you and the hugs of the rain. Stand strong with your bare feet on the ground and with everything that comes from it. Be smarter every day by listening to your intuition, looking at the world with your forehead. Jump, dance, sing, so that you live happier. Heal yourself, with beautiful love and always remember... You are the medicine.» - María Sabina

CHAPTER 20

CONCERNS ABOUT THE WORLD AND 10-YEAR PEACE TREATY PROPOSAL

AN EMERGENCY CALL TO ACTION

An emergency call to action for organizations, leaders, nations and all of humanity.

I would like to ask for a heartfelt request for a 10-year peace treaty for all of humanity .

DEAR ESTEEMED LEADERS of the World and all of humanity,

I write to you today with a sincere and humble request, one that transcends religious, non-religious, political, and non-political boundaries, races, and any idea of separation. I ask all leaders, and all of humanity regardless of their beliefs or affiliations, to join together in a 10-year peace treaty dedicated to uplifting humanity and providing peace and a minimum standard of living for all life.

In this plea, I humbly ask for peace and the provision of essential living conditions for every individual within your respective nations. Basic needs such as shelter, food, water, electricity, internet access, and first necessary supplies must be guaranteed to ensure the survival and well-being of all citizens. Let us foster an environment where every human being can flourish and thrive.

With love and hope for a world at peace. LOVE has already won!

For all the oppressed countries at war, in fear, in suffering. I ask for PEACE, FREEDOM, and LIBERATION. I wish that for all of humanity freedom for all my heart stands with you my brothers and sisters from all walks of life.

DEAR RESPECTED Leaders of All Nations and 8 billion leaders of the world,

I write to you today with a deep sense of urgency and concern regarding the war and how it can escalate to nuclear war that may or may not occur. In the face of this possible danger, I humbly request your participation in a 10-year peace treaty that aims to safeguard our collective future and preserve the well-being of generations to come.

The time to come together as one is now the grand rising and awakening is now, there is no more time to wait. I call on 8 billion leaders of this world to risespeak up and stand for LOVE. Recall Plato's allegory of the cave, where the liberation from fear and illusion led to enlightenment and the birth of a new reality.

The possibility of a nuclear conflict casts a dark shadow upon our planet, holding the power to devastate entire nations and irreversibly harm the delicate fabric of humanity. The consequences of such a war would be catastrophic, not only in terms of immediate destruction but also for the long-lasting impact on the environment, the multiverse, our global community, and the hopes and dreams of future generations.

Recognizing the gravity of this situation, I implore all nations to work proactively and set aside their differences and join forces in the pursuit of peace. Let us commit to a comprehensive treaty that prohibits the use of nuclear weapons, war and destruction. By doing so, we can create a safer and more secure world for ourselves and for the children who will inherit our legacy.

It is crucial that we understand the interconnectedness of our actions and decisions. The effects of a nuclear war or any war, terror, and suffering would extend far beyond individual nations, permeating borders and boundaries to impact the entire planet. The potential loss of innocent lives, the destruction of our environment, and the long-term consequences for global stability are too grave to ignore. It is incumbent upon all of us, as leaders and stewards of our nations, to prevent this possibility from becoming a reality.

In this treaty, I propose that we commit to peace, focusing our efforts on the pursuit of balance, diplomacy, and cooperation. Let us prioritize dialogue, negotiation, and the resolution of conflicts through peaceful means. By redirecting our resources and energy away from the production of weapons and toward the promotion of biodiversity, education, healthcare, sustainable development, regenerative agriculture and the well-being of our citizens, we can create a world where peace flourishes.

Furthermore, I invite all nations to actively engage in

fostering understanding, empathy, and cultural exchange. Let us build bridges of friendship and collaboration, celebrating our diversity and finding common ground amidst our differences. Through mutual respect and open dialogue, we can pave the way for lasting peace and create a future where the scars of war are healed and replaced by the bonds of cooperation and unity.

I understand the challenges that lie ahead and the complexities of international relations and much more information I do not understand from historical and past events leading up to where we are now. However, I firmly believe that our collective commitment to peace can transcend past, present, and future timeliness, political and religious ideologies, historical grievances, and personal ambitions.

Together, we have the power to break the chains of fear, animosity, and mistrust, forging a new path towards a world free from the constant threat of war, destruction, fear, nuclear devastation, any form of enslavement, and anything else other than peace, love and collaboration.

Furthermore, I invite the Vatican, governments, leaders worldwide, the indigenous, aboriginals, men, women, and children and all 8 billion humans to unite in this cause, setting aside religious differences and political ideologies for the greater good. It is not merely about your God or my God, but about all of us—our shared humanity and our planet. I kindly request that any sacred texts and knowledge currently held secret from the rest of humanity be made public. The time has come to embrace the truths about the multiverse, other life forms, our divinity, and the hidden information that have gone unnoticed by many. Why would we continue to enslave our brothers and sisters when we are interconnected as one, we are only enslaving ourselves in the end, there is no separation we are ONE! Can we not recognize the abundance of the multiverse, knowing that there is more than enough for everyone? Together, we can create and collaborate, offering value to one another and creating our individual and collective reality in love, peace, and harmony.

Let us strive for transparency, shedding light on the mental manipulation and enslavement that often goes unnoticed. Fear is an illusion, external and crafted to control us. Instead, we can choose peace, harmony, love and abundance in our world. We possess immense power to shape our realities as active co-creators and fractals of Source, alter our contracts, and transform our Karma to Dharma. Do not underestimate the incredible strength, power and knowledge that lies within us.

We have the potential to change the world and embark on a journey into a new golden age, a new earth that is our birthright, our freedom, and our collective choice. If you have been lead as part of your soul's mission here on earth to perform grid work, hold space, heal, transcend, share knowledge, and more I call on each and every one of you to step into your true power and soul mission.

In this heartfelt request, I yearn for love, humanity, transparency, hope, and compassion to prevail. Let us rise above our differences, embrace our shared destiny, and create a world where every individual can thrive, grow, and live in harmony.

May this plea reach the depths of your hearts, and may the wisdom of compassion guide your decisions. Together, we can transcend borders, ideologies, and limitations to build a brighter future for humanity.

I urge you, esteemed leaders, to consider the weight of our responsibilities and the impact of our decisions on the lives of billions. Let us seize this opportunity to be the architects of peace and champions of a better tomorrow. Our future generations are counting on us to make the right choices.

May wisdom, compassion, and a shared vision guide our actions as we embark on this journey toward lasting peace.

I would love to meet with all leaders of the world to assist me in promoting this request. If there is a way you can help and promote this please do so even if it's by sharing, signing and supporting the petition. If you would like to get in touch directly please email me.

With heartfelt sincerity,

Rosalía

Quantum Alchemist Master™

Write to me via the contact page at QuantumAlchemist-Now.com

«The greatest victories are those won without lifting a sword; for the true battles lie not in the strength of arms, but in the resilience of the human spirit.» - Eleanor Roosevelt.

CHAPTER 21

LOVE HAS ALREADY WON!

YOU ARE NOT A VICTIM,
BUT AN ALCHEMIST

L OVE HAS ALREADY WON! You are not a victim, but an alchemist.

«The most important thing is to figure out what is the most important thing.» - Suzuki Roshi

WE ARE ETERNAL SOULS, multidimensional beings having a human experience, experiencing a different aspect of ourselves, we are a fractal of Source and Source itself, we are the universe, the galaxies and everything that exists, we are ONE. Every life event has prepared you to awaken to come into your power, to your divine being of love.

«Every single thing no matter what it is, is helping to move you to higher and higher levels of self-love» - Credit to the author unknown to me at this time.

WE ARE an all expansive beings in continuous change and transmutation, we are energy in motion, consciousness in action. Every experience is just building blocks in our expansion process. As earth is a planet of perceived polarities, we experience many things to know the other spectrum is also possible, however there is no duality, underneath it, there is only the appearance of it. When is enough, enough? How much longer are we, as a collective, willing to accept this as our reality? Look within, face the dark and light within yourself, integrate the two, find that balance and integration. Find your peace, your freedom. Let's create the new earth together as ONE!

«Any thought of love uplifts the vibration of the universe.»
- Marianne Williamson

Find your own voice, whose voice are you listening to? Your parents, grandparents, the news, society? Your heart has the answers you seek. How many times have we chased love, have looked for love outside of ourselves? In our parents, in partners, in religion, in any environment that would accept us and love us for who we are? How long have we sought outside for approval, love and validation? Our essence is love. Once you arrive at zero point you find that you are whole, that you are perfect as you are, there is nothing to do, nothing to be.

«If we want the world to change, it has to start inside the human soul.» - Michael Meade

From this place of stillness, knowing we are love, consciousness, awareness, we begin to create and expand from our hearts in alignment with our souls, with Source in harmony with the universe in unison as ONE!

Being in your heart center will keep you grounded in who you really are and get you through all seasons of your journey. You don't chase, you attract your vibrational match. The chase is an illusion. Who are you now and who are you becoming in the present moment?

From my perspective love is God and God is love.

«The way of the miracle-worker is to see all human behavior as one of two things: either love, or call for love.» - Marianne Williamson

I believe we, along the Millenia, have caused that division and separation from oneness, from Source. I believe Source is the fabric of the universe, everything is Source itself expressed in different forms but ultimately all made from the same point of origin. The life force, as Source itself in this case, having a human experience. We create and indoctrinate personas and other masks and ideas about ourselves and forget who we are at our core, forget our true essence and divinity. You are worthy, as you are Source itself experiencing itself through you. Practicing self-love and self-forgiveness will begin to remind you of your true essence.

We are here to expand in every possible way, we continue

expanding our consciousness, our awareness, our species and all of our being.

> «When we no longer know what to do, we have come to our real work and when we no longer know which way to go, we have begun our real journey.» - Wendell Berry

I invite you to become the observer of what you are experiencing as a journey of expansion, as consciousness becomes aware of itself in the ever-present now moment. Look at it as being there to be experienced, felt, processed and integrated for the next level of expansion. Look at it from a bird's eye view from the zero point or a point of neutrality, not as being good or bad but just being. We are here to experience a variety of emotions like the rainbow, it's kind of boring just one color so we want to experience the multi color, multi verse of our infinite being. Now we can bring awareness to how we process what we are experiencing, how we react to it, our thoughts, our habits, and actions. How we approach challenges and lessons. How long we stay and in any one particular emotion. Will you stay 10 years in judgment, resentment, hate, guilt, or any other state? This will only harm you. Allow yourself to feel and process the emotions as they show up in the journey but learn to let go, use them as stepping stones, look at the silver lining. How can you alchemize it in the long term for your highest good and let go of what no longer serves you? Everything is transient and in constant change, whatever it is, it will not last forever, let it go!

When we realize that love is the essence of who we are

we begin to practice being grateful, being more forgiving, and understanding of self and others. We detach to who we should be and remember who we are. We let go of chasing and controlling.

«Enlightenment is not a fixed end-it is a timeless movement in love» - J. Krishnamurti

Always come back to your heart center, to the knowing of who you are. Embody your feminine and masculine, your Ying and Yang, your Isis and Osiris, your Shiva and Shakti, your divinity and your true essence. Raise now Gods and Goddesses of the universe and remember your true nature. Live from your heart, your intuition, and your uninterrupted connection to Source and all that exists. That is the birthright of all of us, we can all do it! Stop the outside distractions and listen, shhhh.... Listen closely to the whisper..... of your own mastery.... The answers lie within, go take a deep dive and don't be afraid of yourself, of your own power and divinity.

What if we have already been many things and have experienced ourselves in infinite possibilities and fractals of the divine? What if there was no religion but love, energy and vibration? What if we have been all the elements, earth, fire, water, and air? That we have been light, darkness and every color. That we have been from many planets and many star systems and galaxies and still are. That we have been animals and humans and many other forms and still are? That we have been male and female, that we have been the murderer and the murdered. That we have done things we thought we would never do in this lifetime and others. That we have been through millions of lifetimes and processes of death, rebirth, contraction and expansion? That we have felt all range of emotions and experiences and we simply have forgotten the veil of forgetfulness? Which is starting to lift in each of us. That we have volunteered to come here to Earth at this time with a purpose?

As I remember everything I have been, I look back and have love, compassion and forgiveness for myself and others. I try to keep judgment to the bare minimum even when I'm triggered. For like Jesus said:

«Father, forgive them, for they don't know what they are doing.»

We are not only human, we are not only spirit, we are everything and everything is us, we are ONE! We are consciousness becoming aware of itself, we are Source experiencing creation in infinite forms. The harm I do to another I do to myself, the love I give to another I give to myself. We are unique expressions of the divine, we are all made from the fabric of the universe and we are the universe. I invite you to become the alchemist of your life, build it, design it how you want, as this will have a ripple effect not only in those around you and the collective, but in the multiverse, in the micro-cosm and macro-cosm, parallel, past, present and future lives. Stay centered on the importance of the eternal, ever present, now moment, if time and space didn't exist, all that would exist would be the now, in infinite forms. Look within for whatever is true for you. Self-inquiry will open many doors to your inner wisdom. What life are you choosing to create now? We are taking consciousness to the next level, continuing the expansion process, pushing every limit because there is none. We have the love and support from the universe, mother earth, other planets, galaxies, star systems, motherships, masters, guides, we are fully loved and supported in this process of expansion. Find freedom and mastery within yourself, look within to the depths of your soul and awaken and remember your infinite being, awaken from this matrix and the illusion of separation, remove the veil, find your own truth.

«Spread love everywhere you go. Let no one ever come to you without leaving happier.» - Mother Teresa

As we each begin to awaken, we will each start to lift our own corner, our own perspective of the veil of forgetfulness. Your perspective and what you are shown may be different and unique and that is just perfect the way it is for your path of evolution. We each walk our own path and not one path is alike but we are all walking together in unison in a unified field. We are each playing our own instrument that has its own vibration, frequency and music and adds to the universal symphony we all play together. We are each contributing to a greater divine plan. So can we open up to being more receptive to holding different perspectives and different focus points? Can we zoom out of our individuality and our egos and see the greater picture of union and inter-connectedness of it all and then have the ability to zoom back in and integrate our egos, our darkness and our light and all that we are without judgment? Let's be mindful and respectful of other beings, of what they need for their own path of evolution, not forcing the awakening upon another or our perspectives. We may share our perspectives with the world from our hearts, but it is up to others to perceive, interpret, discern and integrate into their lives.

«Our ability to reach unity in diversity will be the beauty and the test of our civilization.» - Mahatma Gandhi

I have mentioned the word «purpose» many times in this book and after much searching for my own purpose, I have come to find a very simple answer: to give and receive love while expanding my consciousness and my love. Can we agree on what we do want as a collective? Do we want more love, peace, harmony, joy, happiness, passion, respect, and a safe space and freedom to express as our most authentic selves and be able to coexist in harmony with all forms for now and infinity? Everyone outside of you is you for infinite lifetimes and in infinite expressions so you can experience all aspects of creation in the eternal present now-moment from the micro to the macro. You are all of it and so I'm I, from the plant kingdom, to the mineral kingdom, to the cosmos and the multiverse to humanity WE ARE ALL GOD/UNI-VERSE/SOURCE. It is the greatest honor to walk alongside you for all of eternity.

«We are consciousness in human expression.» - Rosalía Quintana, «We are LOVE we are ONE! Will you choose LOVE?»

THANK YOU

Dear Readers,

   With profound gratitude, I stand before you, touched by the beautiful support and love that I have received around this book. What was once a mere dream has blossomed into a reality to be shared with you all. I am deeply humbled by the way you've embraced my work and the warmth with which it has found a home in your hearts. Despite our differences in ideas, beliefs, points of views and so on you have managed to find in your hearts the underlying message of loving and respecting one another as one.

   Being a student and spiritual teacher is a profound calling, one that fills my being with purpose and wonder. Your readership has been a wellspring of inspiration on this remarkable journey. Your willingness to embark on this profound exploration of spirituality and life alongside me fills me with boundless joy. Your open hearts and curious minds, ever receptive to the wisdom I've shared, reaffirm my faith in the remarkable power of human connection and our collective quest for continuous growth and expansion.

   Your messages, your shared insights, and the stories you've entrusted me with have been a constant source of motivation and enrichment. The knowledge that my words have resonated with you, adding a positive brushstroke to the canvas of your lives, touches me to the core and fuels my desire to continue sharing the teachings that hold profound meaning for me. Your thought-provoking questions have challenged me to dive deeper into the realms of spirituality and life, and for that, I am deeply grateful. We are walking and learning together.

I extend a heartfelt invitation to each of you to deepen our connection. Your support has been an anchor on this journey, and I yearn for us to continue this extraordinary voyage together.

You can find me on Instagram at @Quantumalchemistmaster, where we can engage on a more personal level. Explore our website, Quantumalchemistmaster.com, for complementary resources, courses, and much more. Feel free to reach out to me via email at that page.

I would love to hear your thoughts on the book and journey alongside you as you navigate your own spiritual awakening.

Let us navigate the mysteries of life together, knowing that our connection is a testament to the boundless beauty of human connection and universal LOVE.

With gratitude,

Rosalía Quintana

www.ingramcontent.com/pod-product-compliance
Lightning Source LLC
Chambersburg PA
CBHW051148120626
46547CB00012B/995